REAL
EVANGELISM

REAL EVANGELISM

GETTING THE CHURCH BACK TO
EFFECTIVE SOUL-WINNING

EXPOSING EVANGELISM'S SUBTLE
SUBSTITUTES

DR. BAILEY E. SMITH

THOMAS NELSON
Since 1798

NASHVILLE   DALLAS   MEXICO CITY   RIO DE JANEIRO

Published in Nashville, Tennessee, by Thomas Nelson. Thomas Nelson is a registered trademark of Thomas Nelson, Inc.

Thomas Nelson, Inc., titles may be purchased in bulk for educational, business, fundraising, or sales promotional use. For information, please e-mail SpecialMarkets@ThomasNelson.com.

Unless otherwise noted, Scripture quotations are from the KING JAMES VERSION of the Bible.

Scripture quotations noted NKJV are from THE NEW KING JAMES VERSION. Copyright © 1979, 1980, 1982, Thomas Nelson, Inc., Publishers.

978-0-7180-2972-2 (SE)

Library of Congress Cataloging-in-Publication Data

Smith, Bailey E.
    Real evangelism / Bailey E. Smith.—Rev. ed.
       p. cm.
    Includes bibliographical references.
    ISBN 978-0-8499-3778-1 (tp)
    1. Evangelistic work. I. Title.
    BV3790.S63 1999
    269'.2—dc21   99–16381
                                                          CIP

Printed in the United States of America

12 13 14 15 16 QG 7 6 5 4 3 2 1

CONTENTS

Foreword   vii

Preface   ix

Acknowledgments   xi

1. The Dangers of Deceptive Discipleship   1

2. Shallow Living from the Deeper Life   22

3. Coming and Going to Nowhere   37

4. Reservoirs of Truth or Rivers of Blessings?   50

5. Cultivation During Harvest Time   63

6. Theoretical Earnestness Without
   Committed Work   75

7. The Ineffective Right Way of Doing Nothing   88

8. Cultural Heat Without Spiritual Light   96

9. The Tired Pastor and the Weary Lord   106

10. Counting Heads Instead of Changing Lives   124

11. Jesus Excitement Without
    Christian Commitment   137

12. The Power of Proper Priorities   154

13. A Heart Hot for Souls   171

A Must-Read Addendum   177

Notes   183

FOREWORD

Bailey Smith has written a book that will stand the test of time. Recently I had the privilege of visiting with this great preacher and recalled taking my sons to one of his meetings in my hometown when they were boys. His message made an impact in their lives and I believe *Real Evangelism* will make a lasting impression in the hearts of all who read it. Focusing on what the Bible teaches about Christ's followers being soul winners, Dr. Smith outlines the dangers of having our testimony tarnished by Satan's clever tactics that lead to the busyness of activity rather than the command of living and proclaiming the truth and power of the Gospel. This is a book for every believer in Christ to put into action. His emphasis on prayer is power-packed: "Prayer puts spiritual powers in motion. . . . prayer, then, is to be used to awaken the saved to the lostness of the lost." I pray that *Real Evangelism* will awaken your heart and lead

you into the effective personal ministry of winning lost souls
to Jesus Christ.

FRANKLIN GRAHAM
President & CEO
Samaritan's Purse
Billy Graham Evangelistic Association

PREFACE

This book is written to encourage the priority of evangelism. It is not a book designed to be critical of any emphasis in the church but to point out that when these other things are done at the cost of reaching others for Christ, they are used as substitutes for the primary task before us.

The reason, then, for the word *subtle* being used so often is to express that, because each of these other things is good, we can be fooled into believing they are best and final. Most of the substitutes within themselves are good, but they are not good as substitutes for evangelism. Yet, they are becoming that, and the trend is extremely dangerous and very damaging to the fulfillment of the Great Commission. Real and lasting evangelism must be the goal of every church if we are to change our world.

You see, the work of evangelism is our most difficult task. The weakness of the flesh and Satan join together to get us to comfort ourselves with the feeling that, when we are involved in other endeavors, we are doing well. The devil provides substitutes in subtle ways, and we gladly receive them, hoping to relieve our guilt for not being involved in leading others to know Jesus. Millions have fallen victim to that process! This book is to encourage every reader to get busy about real evangelism.

My prayer is that *Real Evangelism* will awaken all who read it to a new joy in sharing their faith. If this happens, the purpose of this book will have been fulfilled.

BAILEY E. SMITH, President
Real Evangelism, Inc.
Atlanta, Georgia

ACKNOWLEDGMENTS

I want to express my deep appreciation for the work of Dr. Alvin Reid, professor of the Bailey Smith Chair of Evangelism at Southeastern Seminary in Wake Forest, North Carolina, for his very meaningful update to this book. He added much to its depth and application for our contemporary society. Dr. Reid is a leading authority in evangelism and church growth today. I am extremely appreciative of his friendship, his commitment to Christ, and his significant help in making this volume all that it is.

1

THE DANGERS OF DECEPTIVE DISCIPLESHIP

There is a strong emphasis now on discipleship in churches and even in denominational programs. This is one of the most dangerous substitutes because it sounds good. One can hear phrases from disciples such as, "We care enough to spend time with the new convert." "We are like the marines; we just want a few good men." "Quality is more important than quantity." "Jesus spent his time primarily with just a few men."

Now, please note that the chapter title indicates *deceptive* discipleship. Obviously, I couldn't be opposed to making disciples because that is exactly what my whole life has been dedicated to doing, and that is what our Lord told us to do. Yet the general approach to discipleship has given many who lean away from soul-winning a haven complete with respectability. In fact, the spirit communicated by hundreds with whom I have had contact is a self-righteous one that looks down on those who have an aggressive concern for the lost. They say, in so many words, "You may be doing more, but I'm doing better."

You see, such an approach becomes a substitute. It causes two important features of Christianity—soul-winning and spiritual growth—to become adversaries when in fact they are friends. The greatest discipleship you can do is to get out and tell others about Jesus. It is not either/or; it is both/and! What are the dangers of this distorted concept of discipleship that avoids real evangelism?

IT IS ESTABLISHED ON A WRONG THESIS

The thesis is really twofold: Jesus spent his time training the Twelve to carry out his message, and if we spend much time with only a few, they will become disciples. Now, let's look at these two strands of thought.

It is true that Jesus chose twelve men to be his special friends and helpers as recorded in Matthew 10:2–4. It is also true that if he chose them to be the hope of his kingdom on earth, he was a miserable failure. After three years of being discipled (to use the current but erroneous thought), they all fled when he really needed them. Jesus apparently knew that such cowardice was present among the apostles; just moments before the Roman soldiers were to come after him, he took three of his closest and most trusted disciples, Peter, James, and John, with him to pray among those eight gnarled olive trees of the Garden of Gethsemane. Please note, as chronicled in Matthew 26:36–46, that even though Jesus took with him the finest he had, those who had experienced the best training that he could give, three times they went to sleep in direct disobedience when Jesus so desperately needed their support.

These disciples had seen Jesus heal the blind with spittle. They had seen multitudes fed with just a morsel of food. They had heard his finest teachings and had observed his most spectacular miracles. They had just come from the intimate fellowship of the Last Supper in the Upper Room, where they heard him say, "For this is my blood of the new testament, which is shed for many for the remission of sins" (Matt. 26:28).

Apparently, this is why Jesus used the direct personal pronoun *you* in verse 40. When he found them asleep, he said with a note of shock and disappointment, "What, could [you] not watch with me one hour?" That is, "Above all people, you who have been with me and seen me and heard me publicly and privately and have known me in the intimate hours of our close fellowship with the Twelve, and yet, you have been caught asleep at this needy time of my life." The result of their going to sleep three times was his final remark to them: "Sleep on." Only two verses beyond this is recorded the drama of Judas's coming with the torchbearing crowd to betray and arrest the Lord. Three of Jesus' disciples refused to watch or pray with him and another disciple led a rabble of enemies to apprehend him—what pitiful representatives of the kingdom.

Then, of course, when Jesus had been arrested and his sentencing had been decreed, only one disciple stood by— John. The years of teaching and training produced Peter, the denier; Judas, the betrayer; James and John, the disobedient sleepers; James, the son of Alphaeus who did nothing worth telling, as was true of another called Simon, the Canaanite; Thomas, the skeptic, and five others who hid for fear of sacrifice when faced with the realistic demands of discipleship.

What are we to conclude from these strange results of taught and nurtured disciples? We obviously cannot conclude that Jesus didn't know the men he chose or that he was a poor judge of character. Neither can we conclude that the life and teachings of Jesus were so unimpressive as to totally uninspire his dearest friends and closest observers.

The conflict comes when we try to make too much of the place of the disciples in the life of Jesus. They were extremely important to him, but the entire future of his work did not rest upon their performance. That future rested in his own life and purpose upon this earth. Much of what Jesus did during his ministry was done apart from the twelve disciples. He also spent much time with the multitudes.

For instance, immediately after the disciples were chosen, the Bible says Jesus sent them out, and "he departed thence to teach and to preach in their cities" (Matt. 11:1). The disciples are not mentioned again for several chapters. It just is not true that had the twelve disciples failed, Christianity would have been buried. Not on your life! A while back, someone wrote a book about Southern Baptists called *God's Last and Only Hope*. Friend, we are not God's last hope, but he is our only hope! Even when Jesus sent his disciples out two by two, those he sent out were not the Twelve, but as Luke 10:1 records, they were an additional seventy disciples. Time and time again, the Scriptures say that Jesus taught the multitudes. Matthew 4:23 reports that Jesus "went about all Galilee." Verse 25 of that chapter says, "And there followed him great multitudes of people from Galilee, and from

4

Decapolis, and from Jerusalem, and from Judaea, and from beyond Jordan."

In other words, many loved and followed Jesus whose names and acts of discipleship we are never told. Even after the Cross, Acts 1:15 tells us, 120 disciples were gathered together. Who can say that some of the most aggressive missionary work was not done by many that loved Jesus and dedicated their life to him, which would have accounted for the apparently cultivated ground into which Peter planted the fruitful seed with his sermon at Pentecost? For indeed, several of the original Twelve are never mentioned again after Acts 1:15. Who carried on that rapid growth of the early church?

It is also interesting that when Jesus decided to teach his most dramatic demands of discipleship, he did not teach them just to a select twelve, but once again, he chose a multitude to reveal his strongest thoughts to concerning what it truly means to be one of his followers. Luke 14:25–33 records his telling the multitude that to be one of his disciples one must hate his father, mother, brothers, and sisters, and his own life also. He must bear his cross and come after Jesus, and he must forsake all that he has. Why then, didn't the Twelve pass those demands of discipleship before the Resurrection?

Here, then, is the danger of current discipleship programs assuming that disciples were made great by meticulous and constant teaching. That is obviously not true. They did come alive from the Resurrection and the Pentecostal effusion. None other than G. Campbell Morgan observed concerning the changed disciples, "In half an hour after Pentecost, they knew more about Jesus Christ than they had ever known before."[1] It wasn't, therefore, the years of training that made them alive because after that training they forsook Jesus. It was after the power of the Holy Spirit dominated their lives. Regarding the disciples, Morgan said:

> Did these men cease to be the friends of Jesus? Surely not. They were still His comrades. Not comrades standing by His side merely, but comrades by identity of life. He was in them. He suffered, and their suffering was His suffering. He rejoiced, and their rejoicing was His joy. He fought, and their fighting was His fighting. That was the great change.
>
> Were they no longer His servants? Surely His servants, but no longer sent from Him, but the very instruments of His own going. Their hands became His hands to touch men tenderly; their feet, His feet, to run on swift errands of God's love; their eyes, His eyes, to flame with His tenderness; themselves part of Himself.
>
> This is mysticism, Christianity is mysticism. But if it be mysticism, it is fact. He is not scientific, it is not honest, to deny the mysticism, until you can otherwise account for the fact. Take the men, the fact of themselves, the changed outlook, the changed behaviour, the moral regeneration, the moral passion, the uplifting fervour, and account for it in any other way.[2]

That's it exactly. That's where modern discipleship has missed the point. It has maintained the didactic skeleton of Christian thoughts and lost the heart that puts life into the body. Therefore, one of the grave dangers of the new school of discipleship is that it is built on the erroneous foundation that the Twelve were the hope of Jesus for world redemption and that much teaching and time bring great dedication.

Other fallacies of this kind of thinking will be seen as we examine the other dangers of deceptive discipleship.

IT IGNORES INDIVIDUALITY

It would certainly be safe to say that the kind of discipling Jesus did never robbed his followers of their individuality, for some of their rough edges remained. Philip was still cautious and conservative. Andrew was yet timid. Peter was certainly vacillating. Judas was the stingy one. But again and again, Jesus used these personality traits to benefit the kingdom's message. Peter's impulsive nature got him to walk on water as no other person ever has.

It greatly disturbs me to see the sometimes irreparable harm caused by deceptive discipleship. Illustrations of its danger abound, but let me mention just one. A staff member in one of the larger churches of our denomination was committed to the idea of discipleship. He gathered a few people around him and met with them at church early in the morning, late at night, and even in their homes. He even told them that he was their "spiritual leader" (self-appointed) and authority. He hovered over them like a mother hen over her chicks. When he moved to another state, he encouraged several of the people he was discipling to move to this location with him so they could be under his spiritual guidance.

After about fourteen months of this, the results were very alarming. One of the discipled men became heavily involved in drugs. Two gave up the idea of the ministry into which they had once testified of being called and for which they had enthusiasm. Another one became highly critical of his church and spread discord among the congregation. A young couple, over which this young church staff member had exercised such control under the guise of discipling, came near divorce when this fine, handsome husband committed adultery. He later told his pastor that the reason he became so low spiritually that he could do such a thing was because of the so-called discipleship. He said it had robbed him of an expressive joy in his Christianity, which seriously depressed him. He said, "How could I have been so blind? I almost lost everything that's important to me."

You see, his discipler and "spiritual authority" had a bad attitude about the local church. After months and months of association with and near brainwashing by his discipler, the husband became bitter about his church and pastor, which in his discipled mind excused his act of immorality. This is not speculation of what happened; this is from the testimony of the young man himself. He was robbed of the joy of serving the Lord. His joy and enthusiasm had been darkened under the shadow of a lifeless and apparently undisciplined discipler.

The young husband later told his pastor, "Sir, I was almost ruined by what I thought was good for me. I was not even thinking for myself." There was a good conclusion to this, however. After psychologically breaking free from this negative influence, this young man is now faithful to all services of his church and each week is being an aggressive witness for Christ. He has learned about real evangelism.

Is this illustration extreme? If it is, it is because deceptive discipleship is an extreme. A thousand similar stories can be related. I personally have a written record of several hundred.

I have talked with several noted Christian leaders and asked them this question: Did anybody ever disciple you?

Without exception they answered something like this: No, thank the Lord! Had they been subjected to the deceptive discipleship that is so prevalent today, they likely would have been robbed of that special individuality that God has used to great success in their lives. Even the rough spots, anointed by the Holy Spirit, can be used for unique and distinctive accomplishments. When one allows someone to shadow his life as his "spiritual leader" and dominate his thinking, he takes on the quirks, oddities, and idiosyncrasies of his discipler. He becomes a disciple all right—of Tom, Henry, Bill, or Harold, but not of Jesus.

One pastor commented after seeing this aberrant kind of discipleship in his church, "If we get any more disciples, it's going to kill us." In some churches death has indeed been the result. They die from acute claustrophobia—shut up too tightly within themselves.

A man in one part of the nation who is active in what he calls a discipling ministry has produced hundreds of disciples. Even though many of them have good qualities, they all bear his obvious theological error. Every one of them shows the same critical spirit he has about several segments of our Christian practice. What a shame that the Holy Spirit was not allowed to do his special work of grace in their individual lives. Their God-given distinctives have been absorbed by their hovering discipler.

I agree with John F. Havlik: "The Church itself must do the equipping."[3] Charles L. McKay in *The Call of the Harvest* says, "Nothing but a church can stabilize, conserve, and utilize saved people."[4] That's why we have Sunday school, church training, evangelism schools, accountability groups, and so forth. Through the training of the body, the individual

9

can learn and grow in Christ without the suffocating influence of a sincere but mistaken discipler. This way Jesus is, as he should be, the discipler through his church where the Holy Spirit does his sure and certain work.

Read carefully these words from John Havlik, an authority on Christ-centered evangelism: "There is today a great deal of emphasis on discipling as a one-to-one process, to the exclusion of the group or the congregation. The truth is that Jesus had twelve men in his group. It was more than a one-to-one relationship. They all had relationship with their Lord."[5]

I repeat then: One of the dangers of deceptive discipleship is that it ignores individuality. That alone calls for concern, for each person is a unique creation of God.

IT NURTURES SPIRITUAL NAVEL GAZING

Now, let me say again that the total function of a Christian community is to make disciples of Christ. I am for disciple-making. It is the erroneous methods of disciple-making so rampant in our land that bother me and many other observers of this strange phenomenon.

Deceptive discipleship nurtures spiritual navel gazing. If you find yourself in a group interested in discipleship but you never get out of the church to live out your faith, you are more interested in the experiences of being together than in making a difference for Jesus. The constant meeting in small groups studying concepts, listening to tapes, and memorizing Scripture leads the disciple to see himself as a monk of deep learning, disassociating himself from the rest of the world. He leaves behind a hundred opportunities about which a true disciple should be concerned to make his meeting. The meeting, the learning, the listening, and the memorizing become ends within themselves. The danger is in enjoying the experience more than the God who calls us to see him. It is assumed that to gather to study is itself an act of Christian discipleship irrespective of the application to life of the lessons learned. Win Arn, in *How to Grow a Church,* sums it up superbly by saying, "True discipleship means that the disciple has the same goals and objectives as his Master. But being committed to discipleship has an additional dimension in growing churches. Discipleship suggests active involvement."[6]

I conducted a revival meeting a few years ago in a church where this wrong kind of discipleship was prevalent. The group of disciples had their Bibles and notebooks. They met at their special times during the week. But not once did any of them show a genuine burden for the revival or for the lost in the community. None of them ever brought a needy visitor to the services. When the educational director promoted the attendance campaign for Sunday, they spoofed it as being below their mature Christian standards. They were too busy meeting in their cloistered groups to get involved in the total ministry of God's church.

Note again the words of Dr. Havlik:

> I was asked to lead revival services in such a church. The members were people of prayer. They studied their Bibles faithfully. They carefully jotted down notes in the margins of their Bibles when I preached. They practiced a degree of separation from the world that was admirable. But the church had not baptized a single convert in three years. They were good, but good for what?[7]

A story from the life of the great missionary evangelist Hudson Taylor gives a better picture. In June 1865, he was in Brighton, England, so burdened for China's multitudes of lost souls. He sat one Sunday in a smug, self-satisfied congregation and observed "pew upon pew of prosperous, bearded merchants, shopkeepers; demure wives in bonnets . . . , scrubbed children trained to hide their impatience." The smug yet indifferent piety made him sick. Seizing his hat, he left, confessing later to being "unable to bear the sight of a thousand or more Christian people rejoicing in their own security, while millions were perishing for lack of knowledge, [and] I wandered out on the . . . sands alone, in great spiritual agony." On the beach he prayed for just twenty-four laborers to go into the world.

Jesus intended for us to be insulated from the world but not isolated. We are not to be introverted monks, disassociated from the ongoing program of an aggressive evangelistic ministry, but rather we are to be involved in the hurt, aches, loneliness, pain, and disillusionment of a world for whom Jesus died.

Did Jesus make disciples? Certainly! But he didn't do it by just leading them away to hide in the mountains with him to study the Old Testament Scriptures. He discipled them by his own example of doing. John Havlik again speaks straight to the point and helps us to see that what is learned must be applied. Read his words carefully.

The Word becomes the deed, and that actualizes the good news into deeds. That is evangelism. The Star of Bethlehem ran an evangelistic errand on that night of nights. The shepherds heard an evangelistic anthem sung by an angelic choir. Wise men came from the east at the beckoning of the evangelistic star. It was good news. It is good news when a Christian loves an alcoholic up out of his drunken hell. It is good news when some loving Christian teaches the unloved and unloving how to love and be loved. It is good news when a concerned Christian teaches an international person the English language. It is good news when some solid, concerned Christian becomes a "big brother" to some fatherless child in the ghetto. It is good news when Christians begin to apply what they believe to the hurts of humanity. When we practice this kind of Christianity, we are practicing the teachings of Christ. Let the Word become the deed.[8]

All of this involvement is for one purpose—to show people everywhere that the disciples of Jesus Christ are caring and loving and involved. That involvement can open doors of strong evangelistic opportunity. There will be no evangelism behind the cloistered walls of disassociated monasticism.

In the first chapter of Acts there is a perfect illustration of what I'm saying. Before Jesus ascended (v. 9) he talked to his disciples. Disciples so often would rather be discussing some theological issue than really getting about what they know to do. So in verse 6 they asked Jesus, hoping to get involved in a lengthy discussion of an interesting point, "Lord, wilt thou at this time restore again the kingdom to Israel?"

Now please note carefully. Don't miss this! Jesus said, "It is not for you to know the times or the seasons, which the Father hath put in his own power" (v. 7). He ended that discussion very quickly, didn't he? "You don't need to know that," he said. You see, Jesus understood that the disciples did not need more hours with him to learn new ideas and accumulate greater knowledge; they needed to get about the business at hand, which was the evangelizing of a world without Christ.

Instead of answering their question, Jesus told them, in essence, to forget it and then in the very next verse he said: "But ye shall receive power, after that the Holy Ghost is come upon you: and ye shall be witnesses unto me both in Jerusalem, and in all Judaea, and in Samaria, and unto the uttermost part of the earth" (v. 8).

Oh, what an absolutely ideal illustration of my whole point. Jesus told them that they didn't need to know anything new; they just needed to get busy about being witnesses. They were trying to find a substitute for real evangelism and he would have no part of it.

Jesus was a doer of the Word. He didn't come to be a speculative philosopher, but to be a lover and Savior of mankind. His disciples were to be out where the people needed them, not sealed off from the reality of the world discussing the "times or the seasons."

"So, he took them through Galilee on a tour of evangelism," says A. C. Archibald, "that they might learn by *observing him at work.* Then having let them see *by his example,* he definitely organized them and sent those out two by two in all parts of the country."[9] When Jesus called his disciples, he said, "Follow me and I will make you to become fishers of men."[10] (See Mark 1:17.) That is still the call of discipleship today.

Often the misguided discipler will say that God doesn't want us to be out working for him; God wants us to be with him. Then the discipler will tell us that we don't need most of all to talk about God but to God. "We must," he will say, "spend more time alone with the Lord just adoring him, loving him, and praising him."

One time I was pondering such phrases, which I basically agree with, but realized there was always something that didn't ring true with them. My spirit really did not bear witness with those who made such statements. J. B. Tidwell, one of the finest laymen in the world, listened as I tried to figure out what wasn't good about that emphasis. He then told me a most profound thing that made it absolutely clear in my mind. I shall always be grateful to this good Hobbs, New Mexico, friend for his insight.

Mr. Tidwell said, "Preacher, let's suppose I had a ranch and one time I hired a couple of fellows to help me around the place because there was much work to be done. Let's suppose that at 5:30 A.M. the next morning I heard those two men outside my bedroom door singing to me, expressing their affection to me, telling me how much they appreciated the job I had given them, and this went on and on and on. I would get up and say, 'Listen men, I hired you to work. There are fences to be mended, cattle to be rounded up, horses to be broken, hay to cut, and wood to cut. The best way you can please me is to not sit here telling me how much you love me, but to show me by doing the work that's important to me. I'll know by that if you really love me.'" He said, "Do you see, Brother Bailey?"

I said, "J. B., that's it. That's it exactly. The best way to love God is to be about what is important to him, the winning and the loving of men and women and boys and girls to himself."

All of us must have a quiet time, preferably in the morning. We certainly need to have a time of daily Bible study. We do need to get our face before God. And we need to pray and study God's Word with other believers. But all of that is for naught if it doesn't cause us to be more concerned for the needs of a hurting world apart from Christ. Like the rancher, God is best pleased when we are out in the field doing the work we were all saved to do—evangelizing.

Yes, God wants our love, but he knows the difference between devotional idleness and loving action. You can go without loving, but you cannot love without going. Don't be disassociated from the lost and needy.

IT PREVENTS PASSIONATE PROCLAMATION

This thought of monastic disassociation leads me to point out another danger of deceptive discipleship. Many of the disciples involved in this erroneous approach see only the few. They see only the ones being discipled. This prevents the passionate proclamation of the gospel from occurring.

The discipling group becomes almost a club of the select few. The people who get the special discipleship training are the ones already involved to some degree in the life of Christ. Yes, I know that it is the saved person who has to be discipled, but the deceptive discipleship approach often dulls the life of joy and enthusiasm and compassion possessed by the Christian who was won to Christ and involved in the ministry of the church by a conscientious soul-winner.

A youth pastor of a church took the approach of gathering a few young men around him to disciple. For several years they met together time and time again. He was their spiritual leader. However, when the pastor began to check the Sunday school roll of the youth departments, he discovered that more than 80 percent of the absentees had never been visited. Not only had the absentees not been visited by the youth director, but neither had he motivated anyone else to take the initiative to visit them. This was after three years of having an opportunity to do so.

The youth pastor had been meeting with these select men who looked like him, dressed like him, combed their hair like him, lived in homes similar to his, talked like him, and sure enough, they turned out like him. Yet, the young girl enrolled in the eighth-grade department, who lived in the modest frame house at the end of the gravel road and was absent most of the time, never got one word of encouragement or concern from her youth director in three years because he was too busy "discipling." And the senior boy with an alcohol problem, attending one rock concert after another, had been enrolled in Sunday school for four years and did not even know the name of that youth pastor.

In other words, the ones who could have benefited the most from genuine love and compassion were ignored because the one responsible for them was carrying on "a deeper ministry." In the original Greek, there is one good word for that—*bologna!* Just because someone cannot dress like us and go on ski retreats with a few and is unaware of the newest books on making disciples does not mean he or she should be beyond the scope of our love and ministry. How much better if that youth pastor had, in the style of Jesus, taken those young trainees out into the neighborhood where the people were to love them and help them in the name of Jesus.

We cannot separate passion for God from the teaching we receive about him. I have seen believers who were so on fire for God when they met Jesus that they would have taken on hell with a squirt gun! But these dear believers, after getting involved in discipleship programs that discouraged evangelism, lost their fire.

Remember again the words of Archibald stating that Jesus taught his disciples by allowing them to learn "by observing him at work."[11] Jesus was never blind to the needs of the youngest, the poorest, the most sinful, the most distant, or the most difficult. His compassionate, loving vision was as broad as the world.

McGavran speaks to the issue perfectly.

Church-growth men use the word *discipling* to mean the initial step by which people come to Christ and become baptized believers. We go on and say that the second part of church growth is "perfecting" or growing in grace. It's making sure that the baptized believers become biblical Christians, that their lives are irradiated by the knowledge of the Bible, and that they have a deep personal relationship with Jesus Christ.

In America today many Christians are interested solely in perfecting existing Christians and not in finding the lost and discipling them. This is a mistake. Mind you, I am all for Christians being better Christians. We should act more justly, and have more love for each other; nevertheless, no amount of loving each other and treating each other more justly is really going to help the church grow very much. You've got to go out where the lost sheep are. You've got to search for them in the right ravines, then get near them and persuade them to come into the fold. We need both discipling and perfecting. We need to find the lost and help them grow in grace.[12]

Beware of a deceptive discipleship that prevents the passionate proclamation of the gospel. It is not Christlike. The devil uses it as a subtle substitute for real and loving evangelism.

THE MISTAKE OF MULTIPLICATION

When people are around those who have taken this improper approach to discipleship, they hear another danger expressed in the word *multiplication*. Disciplers are slick with phrases such as "We don't need more additions to our churches; we need more multiplication in our churches." Admittedly, this sounds good on the surface, but at closer examination one can see some inherent problems.

Let me first say that I believe in the theory of multiplication evangelism. That is, one wins one who wins another, who wins another, and so on. Certainly all of us should desire to multiply ourselves in winning people to Christ on a one-to-one basis. I not only believe it but I also practice it. The problem with this is that we do not live in a theoretical world but a real world.

The real stinger comes, however, at the point of the conclusions drawn from this approach. The improper disciple believes that if he will just pour himself through teaching into this certain person or people, then that individual or those two or three will, in turn, do the same for others. That, of course, often occurs. But the conclusion that this will result in heartfelt evangelism causing a chain reaction of rapid converts is absolutely wrong. It just does not work. It becomes a subtle substitute for real evangelism.

Here's what happens! The one discipling takes someone

who was won to Christ years before. It's someone he likes and who fits the social, academic picture of a disciple in his opinion. He spends time teaching him how to have a quiet time, how to memorize Scripture, how to be submissive to authority, and how to have a servant attitude. Then the discipled person finds someone else already won to Christ and begins doing the same thing to him. But if the element of strong, aggressive evangelism is left out, faulty discipleship is the result.

If someone without a genuine burden for souls, someone without a desire to win people to Christ, someone not sold out to the work of the local church is discipling, how in the world do you suppose the one being discipled is going to turn out? He will be just like the discipler. If the discipler shows by his own example that all he does is spend time with the one being discipled, he gets the idea that all he has to do is to spend time with someone already won to Christ. If the discipler is not winning people, how can we expect his student to do it? I don't intend to be harsh, but for the sake of communication, let me say in short that if the one doing the discipling is a dud, you don't produce an on-fire disciple, you wind up with two duds. This kind of discipler is really a wall between the disciple and Jesus Christ, blocking the vision the disciple should have of his Lord. That has happened far too often.

Too, there is nothing wrong with additions. After all, one plus one equals two, but one times one is still one. Acts 2:47 says, "And the Lord added to the church daily such as should be saved."

This, I trust, helps to do what I promised earlier—to show that time spent just teaching concepts to a few does not necessarily produce effective evangelists. Frankly, it often becomes a substitute for evangelism. Still, the institutional church, with all of its faults, is God's best method today for producing well-balanced disciples.

Dr. Havlik says it well:

> It is interesting to see that the disciple relationship of persons to Christ in the Gospels is a teacher-pupil relationship. In Ephesians it is the pastor-teacher who has a major role in equipping the saints to do the work of ministry. The word *disciple* in all its forms is used 231 times in the Gospels, 30 times in Acts, and not a single time in the Epistles. This is far too significant to ignore. *The emphasis shifts from the relationship of the believer to Jesus Christ to the relationship of the believer to the church-body.* Remember, it is the body of Christ.[13]

Thus the dangers of deceptive discipleship can be minimized by seeing that our ultimate concern should be to involve everyone possible in the ministry of Christ's body, the church, teaching them to love the lost, train the saved, and experience unspeakable joy. Healthy evangelism will result instead of a subtle substitute.

Dr. C. E. Autrey is exactly right when he says, "It was the purpose of Christ to use His disciples to win the world to himself. Thus, Jesus instituted the church for this definite purpose. He intends that His church shall perform many other tasks, but its supreme task is to bring the lost to Christ."[14]

2

SHALLOW LIVING FROM THE DEEPER LIFE

Another thing that in a very clandestine and subtle way takes the place of real evangelism is an emphasis called the deeper life. Remember that in the preface of this book I said that these subtle substitutes in themselves may often be very good. In the case of the deeper-life emphasis, that certainly applies. However, nothing at all is good that substitutes for or detracts from the purpose for which Jesus died—winning persons to eternal salvation.

Let me hasten to say that this emphasis has been a rich blessing to my life. The writings of Norman Grubb, Andrew Murray, Oswald Chambers, Manley Beasley, and Jack Taylor have given me a better understanding of the Holy Spirit's place in my life. In fact, I say categorically that the teachings of the Spirit-filled life and the so-called deeper life have been a necessity for our carnal age. I thank God for their recent prominence.

As with most good endeavors, however, Satan has gotten involved. Or, maybe Satan has gotten involved in some churches and in the lives of some people who have misappropriated the teachings of the Bible, such as the good authors of the deeper-life thoughts. It was never meant to be a substitute for evangelism but an amplification of evangelism. It was meant to enrich, not to stymie the saved. Here again, however, it has become a subtle substitute for evangelism. Because of the sheer labor involved in successful witnessing, some people are always looking for a place where they can rest short of being an evangelist without feeling guilty. So, they have crawled under the warm blanket of the deeper life and gone contentedly to sleep. Thus shallow living results from the deeper life. What are the indications of such a condition?

RATIONALIZING LAZINESS

From those who have sought the deeper-life emphasis as a refuge from evangelism, one can hear phrases such as "I can't do anything; God does it through me"; "It's not my ability; it's my availability"; "Man can't do anything for God." And then, of course, to add authority to their statements they quote Galatians 2:20: "I am crucified with Christ: nevertheless I live; yet not I, but Christ liveth in me." These statements are not necessarily bad, but they are often quoted to excuse inactivity and to rationalize laziness.

F. E. Marsh says it well:

> There is a spurious holiness which looks at itself with a self-satisfied complacency, and criticizes others with a

23

critical spirit of censure. Such persons need to remember one thing, that whenever the Spirit is said to come upon individuals, he came upon them to communicate blessing to others, and not for the endued to retain blessing for themselves.[1]

One of these super-pious saints said about a well-known preacher friend of mine, "Yes, he wins many people to Christ, but I understand he does it all in the flesh." That is not a new criticism of sincere soul-winners, but it isn't as well challenged as it should be. What in the name of all that's reasonable does that statement mean? One of the most difficult and tiring things on earth is to spend hours getting in and out of an automobile, knocking on doors, and presenting the gospel to the rude as well as to the interested. I remember the days before air conditioning in cars or many homes, when preachers drove me around from 9:00 A.M. until 6:00 P.M. during revivals, trying to win people to Christ. Listen, that is far too hard on the flesh to do it in the flesh. The reason most people *don't* win others to Christ is because of the flesh. They try to pamper their flesh and rationalize their laziness by saying, "I'll let God do it through me." To interpret that in practical terms it means, "I'll sit in my motel room while the soul-winners go out and knock on doors in the flesh. I'm Spirit-filled." Horrible!

Perhaps some of Paul's opponents considered him in the flesh when he shared Christ. But Paul didn't mind because he knew the gospel was too important: Notice what he said in Philippians 1:15–18 (NKJV):

Some indeed preach Christ even from envy and strife, and some also from good will: The former preach Christ from selfish ambition, not sincerely, supposing to add affliction to my chains; but the latter out of love, knowing that I am appointed for the defense of the gospel. What then? Only that in every way, whether in pretense or in truth, Christ is preached; and in this I rejoice, yes, and will rejoice.

Dr. Herschel Hobbs says that a person does not have to advertise the obvious.

Indeed, the person who makes a boast of being filled with the Holy Spirit may contrariwise be filled with inordinate pride. Jesus never boasted of the Spirit's presence in His life. Yet no one will deny such a presence. It showed in His every attitude, word, and deed.

The greatest constructive forces in life are those silent powers which work without ostentation. Gentle breezes do not roar yet they bear pollen from one plant to another, making possible an abundant harvest. Mighty rivers flow gently as they bear the commerce of nations. Tides silently lift ocean liners where groaning machines fail. The brain of Albert Einstein made no noise in its amazing computations, but it lifted man's horizon beyond his fondest dreams.

So the Christian who is filled with the Holy Spirit lets his light "so shine before men, that they may see his good works, and glorify his Father which is in heaven" (Matt. 5:16). This kind of person is God's most effective human instrument in the work of evangelism.[2]

How can you tell if a person is filled with the Spirit? The Scripture gives us clear guidance. First, Jesus said when the

Spirit comes, He will point others to Jesus (John 15:26). It stands to reason then that the Spirit-filled person will do the same. Second, the filling of or leading of the Spirit in Acts almost always leads to the preaching of the gospel.

It is true that when one is filled with the Holy Spirit, the result is seen not in the anointment of its presence but in a life that daily lives the Christ life and brings others to Christ. Notice that Jesus said in the Matthew passage that our light is to let people see our "good works," not our inactivity. The Spirit-filled person is a busy person, who without fanfare to draw attention to his spiritual gifts or qualifications, does the Master's work in his daily life.

When God gets in a person, he comes out of that person. You can no more hide Jesus in a life that's redeemed than you can hide the fragrance of a rose under a hair net. The criticism of the lazy and spiritually flabby has always been "It's done in the flesh." What else do we have to do it in? We are all flesh. I'd rather win people to Christ in my flesh than to have my dormant flesh keep me from it. Hard work, organized visitation, and long hours of evangelistic visitation are not in conflict with the Spirit-filled life. Jesus never put a premium on laziness or idleness. There is no conflict between exertion and faith—none at all.

In a powerful book entitled *War on the Saints,* Jessie Penn-Lewis says passivity is not Christian at all but actually gives room for the devil.

> The chief condition for the working of evil spirits in a human being, apart from sin, is passivity, in exact opposition to the condition which God requires for His working. Granted the surrender of the will to God, with active

choice to do his will as it may be revealed to him, God requires cooperation with His Spirit, and the full use of every faculty of the whole man. In brief, the powers of darkness aim at obtaining a passive slave or captive to their will; while God desires a regenerated man intelligently and actively willing and choosing, and doing His will in liberation of spirit, soul, and body from slavery.[3]

Certainly I've known people who have done good things with carnal motivations, but I have known far more who have refused to do anything, saying they prefer to just "let God speak through them." God speaks better through those who are willing to be totally at his disposal.

In Matthew 10 Jesus commissioned his disciples. Now notice that in verses 6 and 7 he used the word *go* and in verse 16, he said, "I send you forth." This is the chapter where Jesus described the cost of following him and told the disciples that they were to go into the cities and salute the houses and share his message to those that would listen (vv. 11–12). Jesus described a life hard on the flesh in that chapter when he said, "And he that taketh not his cross, and followeth after me, is not worthy of me. He that findeth his life shall lose it: and he that loseth his life for my sake shall find it" (vv. 38–39). Without question strong demands were made upon the physical life of his followers.

Now, don't miss this. In the midst of describing how the disciples were going to have to work, labor, visit homes, experience hatred, bear crosses, all of which are difficult on the flesh, Jesus said, "For it is not ye that speak, but the Spirit of your Father which speaketh in you" (v. 20).

Wow! There it is! Total dedication of the flesh to be an

instrument through whom God speaks. Let me reiterate. There does not have to be a conflict between sensible hard work and the Spirit-filled life. In fact, one is not present without the other. Jesus told his disciples that in their hard work the Spirit of God would speak through them. Undoubtedly, the Spirit will not speak through a lazy, barren, cross-avoiding life. He will not be identified with such hypocrisy. Proverbs says of a slothful man, "He also that is slothful in his work is brother to him that is a great waster" (18:9).

During a recent visit to the Holy Land, our guide told us that often Jesus would walk twenty-one to twenty-five miles per day going about his ministry. He did it in the flesh, obviously, for he was flesh, but he was also God incarnate. The tiring, walking, and working of Jesus did not indicate that he was carnal or unspiritual. It did indicate that he was deeply committed to being in the will of the Father and that he had set his face like a flint toward the ultimate discipline of the flesh, the cross of Calvary.

My friend, if you are one of those who tries to hide from your responsibility to win people to Christ in the illusion that you are more mature than the soul-winner because you have gone deeper than that, I trust that you will see the error of your way. How much deeper can one get than helping men and women, boys and girls to know that Jesus can be their personal Lord and Savior? Neglecting evangelism by saying you're in the deeper life indicates clearly that you are living a shallow life, trying to find a substitute for your genuine need of being an aggressive witness. This is one of the devil's most subtle substitutes. Beware of rationalizing laziness.

C. H. Spurgeon, the genius preacher of England, said,

> It is not at all an easy calling [to be a soul-winner]. He
> does not sit in the arm chair and catch fish. He has to go
> out in rough weather. If he that regardeth clouds will not
> sow, I am sure he that regardeth clouds will never fish. If
> we never do any work for Christ except when we feel up
> to the mark, we shall not do much. We must be always at
> it, until we wear ourselves out, throwing our whole soul
> into the work in all weather, for Christ's sake.[4]

Let it be made clear that the Holy Spirit is not the enemy
of evangelism. He is the agent of evangelism. "No man can
come to the Father unless my Spirit draws him." And the
Spirit is the equipper for the evangelist, but he expects us to
care and go forth. Remember that in Acts 1:8 when the disciples received the Holy Spirit, they were to be witnesses as
a result of that power.

Lewis Drummond says, "God desires his evangelists to
be burdened, concerned, enthusiastic, and zealous to spread
the good news to the millions who desperately need to hear
the message. And this attitude the Holy Spirit will instill as
we seek his strength, wisdom, and compassion."[5]

NO ROOM FOR FAILURE

One of the current techniques of those who have sought
what they call the "deeper life" as a refuge from personal
evangelism is to assume that all that happens is just fine
with God. They tell us not to worry, fret, or stew because
what is happening is in the great providential working of

the Lord. Then, often they add piously, "God knows what he's doing."

A pastor in a southern state had that approach when he stood up to face 150 people in an auditorium that would seat 900. Coming to the pulpit after a few struggling hymns of worship, he said, "Well, we could have had a bigger crowd, I know, but there is one thing that I am convinced of—everybody is here tonight that God wants here."

No! No! No! That can't be true. Just because a church has not planned, advertised, promoted, worked, or visited does not mean that those who show up by default are the only ones God wanted present. *Little work does not automatically mean great spiritual power.* Certainly I realize that promotion is no substitute for God's presence of Holy Spirit power, but I also realize that sloppy handling of God's affairs is no incentive for the Holy Spirit to do his work. Yes, I also know that large crowds do not guarantee great spiritual results but neither do small crowds. Pentecost certainly brought a huge gathering and three thousand converts and a great outpouring of the Holy Spirit fire falling from heaven. That was not bad results. Jesus used the word *compel* when he told us to go into the highways and hedges to bring people into the house of God.

Here again, because evangelism is the most tiring thing we do, comfortable substitutes are sought, even sought subconsciously on occasion. Some good people have taken the emphasis of the deeper life and used it as a pious shield from the harsh realities of a demanding world, saying, *Qué será será*—whatever will be will be. That indeed is a very comfortable position to come to because it alleviates all chances of failure. Therefore, when little crowds and little results and almost no converts are forthcoming, the misguided "deeper-lifer" says (even though little honest, prayed-through effort has been expended), "Well, praise the Lord, God is doing a quality work among the few. I'm not concerned, for this is not my work; it is God's." In effect this approach leaves one in the position to feel that he or she is God's special spiritual super-saint and the fact that people are not being greatly saved can't really matter, for there are other things, you know. Super-saint? Maybe instead, slothful sluggard.

Not until we have done our best can we assume that we will receive God's best. Wasn't it Spurgeon who said, "Work as if everything depended upon us, and pray as if everything depended on God"? That is still a good philosophy for Christian service. Spurgeon profoundly stated, "Prayer and means go together. Means without prayer—presumption. Prayer without means—hypocrisy."[6]

Let's quit trying to find spiritual excuses for our uninvolvement and pray to the Father for a greater concern to take our world for Jesus with an aggressive sense of conquest in the name of Calvary's cross. A steward is to be found faithful, so let's be no less than that as stewards of the message of salvation.

SURRENDER INSTEAD OF VICTORY

Some years back, I found myself at a church as one of the speakers for a Spiritual Life Conference. The experience was most educational. It confirmed in my mind all over again the priority of evangelism in making the church well-pleasing to the Lord.

Several of the deacons and the pastor and I were talking after one of the evening services as we stood under the big oak tree near the auditorium. The discussion began to focus on the past ministry of the church. "The church used to win a lot of people to Christ." "It used to have a successful Sunday school." "It used to have a large attendance in the worship services." "It used to have some exciting and joyful services." "God's power used to fall on the services in mighty displays of his presence through a sense of confession, conviction, and urgency about his work." On and on such statements could be heard that night. There was evidence of a genuine longing for things that used to be.

When the pastor and I got in the car, he said to me, "You know, it's true that when I first came here the church was much larger in Sunday school attendance. I suppose we are less than half now of what we once were. And it did concern me for a while, but I thank the Lord he has given me the victory. It doesn't bother me anymore. I have led the church to see the Spirit-filled life, and that's why we just have conferences like this instead of revivals where you have to plan, promote, and go all out. It's great to have the victory."

In all honesty, when I got back to my motel room, I was sickened to my heart. I got down on my knees beside my bed and prayed something like this, "Lord, if I'm wrong about the place of evangelism, please reveal it to me. I don't want to be off base. I don't want to be lopsided, but, Lord, I can't feel right about what I see here this week. Please make me what you want me to be."

Well, since then I have heard similar conversations proclaiming victory amid declining evangelism and upon close

examination one can see that *it is not victory that is there,
but surrender.* It is surrender to the price of achievement. It
is surrender to the demands of reaching a community with
the gospel. It is surrender to the pressures of administering a
growing flock. It is surrender to the empathy one has to feel
when compassion drives him or her to love the lost in the
name of Jesus. It is surrendering excellence for mediocrity.

Oh, this position is so tempting for all of us because "the
harvest truly is plenteous, but the laborers are few" (Matt.
9:37). It *is* work, it *is* a struggle, it *is* an effort to jump into
the task of world redemption with both feet; and heart, soul,
and life. It cost Jesus an ignominious death on a Roman gib-
bet, but he was willing to pay whatever price was necessary.
The Scriptures remind us that the servant is no better than
his Master. If Jesus could bleed for the salvation of a lost and
dying world, are we too good to sweat for the same?

I cannot say often enough that I am so grateful for the
teaching of the Spirit-filled life. It has genuinely enriched my
life. And as a matter of fact, those who teach it most effectively are some of my dearest friends and agree with me that
it is not to be a substitute for evangelism, for indeed no one
can be filled with the Holy Spirit who is not an evangelist.
Jesus told the disciples where they would go, then he said,
"Lo, I am with you." His presence was nearest when they
were going and sharing.

Victory is not to be found in disobedience to the Great
Commission. Victory is not succumbing to the forces that
would lessen the commitment to the honest demands of discipleship. Victory is not forgetting about the little boys and
girls near you who ought to be reached in love for Bible
study in the Sunday school system of your church. Victory is

not making yourself feel good when you're doing bad. That
is called surrender.

Don't surrender, dear brother. Fight on! Greater is he
that is in you than he that is in the world. Give your best,
and God will give the victory.

WHEN THE BURDEN LEAVES

Closely associated with what I've just said is the apparent
effort that some are making to lose the burden for a lost
humanity. It is not difficult to see why some Christians
would try to substitute a life of floating on the placid pool of
the deeper life for swimming against the swift current of the
world's lostness. To feel a sense of responsibility, to face our
uncaring world with the message of Christ, is an awesome
feeling. In fact, Jesus felt that burden so severely it apparently burst his heart wide open with grief as he hung sus-
pended between heaven and earth on the cross.

"I cannot believe," said Spurgeon, "that you will ever
pluck a brand from the burning, without putting your hand
near enough to feel the heat of the fire. You must have, more
or less, a distinct sense of the dreadful wrath of God and of
the terrors of the judgment to come, or you will lack energy
in your work, and so lack one of the essentials of success. I
do not think the preacher ever speaks well upon such topics
until he feels them pressing upon him as a persistent burden
from the Lord."[7]

Let's not try to escape that burden though it be difficult
indeed to bare. The escape hatch for many has been what
they have incorrectly called the deeper life. They have gone
deep, like the ostrich's head goes deeper into the earth,

blinding themselves to the real world and the real need and the real price. They no longer feel guilty about being guilty—guilty of talking a spiritual language but refusing to share Christ with a lost neighbor. They have become relaxed reclining on the couch of unconcern, growing sluggishly fat through the lack of spiritual exercise. They say, "I've got the victorious life," which means they are not bothered by the fact that God isn't using them anymore.

Once again Jessie Penn-Lewis and Evan Roberts focus in on the problem in an exacting manner. They observe that so many Christians are "craving for comfort and happiness and peace in spiritual things, they have sung themselves into a 'passivity'—i.e., a passive state of 'rest,' 'peace,' and 'joy'—which has given opportunity to the powers of darkness to lock them up in the prison of themselves and thus make them almost incapable of acutely understanding the needs of a suffering world."[8]

As difficult as that burden is for a world without Christ, we must not allow it to escape us. When it leaves, we might emit a sigh of personal relief, but at that moment our life will lose its zeal and contagious enthusiasm for a disciplined life of service. Having the burden does not mean that we will constantly feel weighted down, worried, haggard, and joyless. It does mean that we, like our Lord, will have a daily sense of genuine interest in confronting the lost with God's eternal hope. It means that we will have ever before us the vision of the lostness of men apart from Jesus, willing to be used of the Holy Spirit in loving, caring, and sharing.

That burden led Christ to the cross, but that cross has brought millions to the Christ. Our cross bearing will do the same. Get under that cross of caring and do as Jesus, "who for the joy that was set before him endured the cross, despising the shame" (Heb. 12:2). Arn is right, "To grow in Christlikeness means to share His burden for the salvation of the world."[9] That, indeed, is the Christian life at its best and deepest.

Because the deeper life in its best and truest definition is good, Satan has tried to distort its purpose and make it a subtle substitute for real evangelism. When that occurs, shallow living results in neglect of every Christian's first duty—witnessing. Don't let it happen to you!

If I were on a railroad track, passed out, I wouldn't want you to stand twenty-five yards away and say, "Well, once I would have felt an urgent need to wake that man up and tell him a locomotive is coming, but I don't worry since I've got the victory." No sir! I would want you to arouse me and get me off that track before I was crushed by the train. In fact, it really wouldn't bother me if you were carnal and did it in the flesh. The primary consideration is that my life would be saved.

C. E. Autrey said, "Jesus had but one mission on this earth, and that mission was to seek and to save the lost."[10] Why? Because he saw their danger without a Savior. He saw the iron horse of eternal death rushing to destroy their souls. We all must obtain a new urgency about rescuing all people who are lost, knowing that they are only one heartbeat from hell. Keep the burden and be a blessing.

3

COMING AND GOING
TO NOWHERE

D o you remember hearing of the airplane pilot who came
on the speaker and told his cabin full of passengers,
"Ladies and gentlemen, I want to let you know that my nav-
igational instruments are malfunctioning, and I don't know
where we are or where we are going. However, I want to
encourage you with the fact that we are making excellent
time"?

How accurately descriptive that is of the third subtle
substitute for evangelism I want to discuss with you—the
sometimes meaningless business of the church. Now, I am a
churchman with every ounce of my being, but it doesn't even
take an intelligent observer of modern ecclesiastical motion
to see that much of the coming and going in churches is
unproductive. We apparently don't know where we are
headed, but we're making such excellent time we just hate to
question our course.

Let's examine some of the ways in which our coming and going have led us away from the primary task of evangelism.

FERVOR OR FEVER?

Fervor! That's a good word, even a good preacher word. It has the golden sound of activity, zeal, dedication, involvement, and ardor. All of us would hope that someone could speak of our noticeable fervor. Church members around the globe are encouraged to show undaunted fervor in their Christian pilgrimage, which, without question, is a worthy admonition. But how that fervor is to be expressed in meaningful ways—genuinely Christlike ways—is the ultimate question.

This self-interrogation to gain a proper perspective in regard to our busy church activities can be aided by asking the right questions. Church members should ask themselves: Am I doing what I'm doing for social reasons only? Do I just want to eat at the potluck supper, shake the hands, and have the fellowship? Does this really have a deeper meaning to me than attending a civic club function or a country club party? Could I be subconsciously feeling that my crowded church schedule indicates that I have the frisky fervor that eliminates my responsibility to get busy about the purposeful work of Christ?

The people I love in a special way are our older people— those whom the years have given the furrowed brows and silver hair—the senior citizen, if you please. But they need a word of challenge as much as any group in the church I know. Far too often when people pass fifty, they start saying things like, "Let the younger ones do it; I've done my part." So they attend the "Golden Age" club at church. They just love the

"Jolly Sixties" group. They even attend churchwide functions that demand no more than fun and fellowship. They have assumed that age excuses them from the deep spiritual functions of the church, especially in the matter of evangelism.

My older friends, let me give you a very personal word of encouragement. When Paul wrote the book of Philippians, he was in jail, a prisoner. He was also past sixty-three years of age. But he said with an eye toward a determined and worthwhile future, "Forgetting those things which are behind, and reaching forth unto those things which are before, I press toward the mark for the prize of the high calling of God in Christ Jesus" (Phil. 3:13–14).

Even at sixty-three and after a life of unparalleled Christian achievement, Paul said that the laurels of the younger years were good but he was looking forward to a more profitable future. You can and should have the same attitude.

I have discovered that nursing homes, clubs for the aging, and special communities for the retired are filled with lost people nearer eternal judgment than the average citizen. Older people, the church needs your wisdom, your accumulated knowledge, your gracious personalities, and your more relaxed schedules to go to these areas and present the gospel of a saving Christ to these sweet and nice, but lost, older folks. Don't for a minute think that you're one of the old saints of the church just because you've spent a few decades on planet earth. Age does not automatically mean spiritual maturity; it might mean years of increasing backsliding. I know you may be limited by declining health, but if you were to take your hot fever for the social activities and use that in true evangelistic fervor, there is no telling what you

could get done for eternity. I propose to you that your best
years for Christ are in your future, not in your younger and
more vigorous past.

I think the slogan of some churches ought to be, "Meet it,
eat it, and beat it." The crowd gathers, the food is eaten, and
the benediction pronounced. Over and over that process is
repeated, but one wonders if that is all there is. Motion without meaning. Remember, the fastest chicken in the chicken
yard is the one with his head cut off! Make sure all of your
business results in people coming to know Christ. A pastor
friend of mine called me one day and told me that a group of
his ladies was doing a mission action project. I said, "Great,
what is it?" He said, "They have decided to make covers for
tissue boxes at the nursing homes. I was hoping," he said,
"that they would get about some real evangelistic efforts."

Yes, I know that people can be reached through efforts
such as that. I also know that too often such activities
become substitutes for soul-winning. A lady on her way to
hell can crochet a cover for a facial tissue box, but a lady
with Jesus in her heart should do something more. Yes, do
good and helpful things for others, but if you never get
around to sharing Christ with them, you are disobedient to
the Word of God.

Be busy for eternity. Have a fervor that compels you to
give a witness to everyone possible. Deal with your own lack
of compulsion to be the evangelist you ought to be. Ask
yourself why you would rather cook a meal for a bereaved
friend than share Jesus. A Buddhist can take a pie to a home
where there has been a death, but while a Christian ought to
do the same, a Christian must do infinitely more.

Fever can make you warm, but real fervor comes from

being on fire. Young, middle-aged, and the elderly, let's get hot on the trail for souls. Certainly, be faithful to your meetings but become a catalyst that will cause a reaction of renewed purpose in the life of your church. Instead of just being busy, why not determine to bring a blessing? In our society that is so fast-paced, we act as though being busy is a sign of spiritual maturity! But in all our busyness, are we really affecting eternity?

One year I attended the state fair in Dallas, Texas, where I observed a most interesting exhibit in the science building. As I approached the crowd gathered around this particular exhibit, I noticed that as each one was leaving, having gazed long enough, he or she wore a strange smile. When I got to where I could really see, I understood why. There was a machine that seemed to have everything—pistons, gas jet with ball bouncing up and down, chain, locomotive arms going back and forth—and it was beautifully chromed. Every part was moving, and it was so well engineered that it did not make one sound. Where did the strange smiles come from? They came because of a little sign at the base of the machine: "It doesn't do anything, but my, doesn't it work well!"

Do I really need to apply that? One of the devil's most subtle substitutes for evangelism is to get church people so busy with the fever of coming and going to meetings that they never make one dent in Satan's armor. Dear reader, don't be guilty of working well and doing nothing. Be eternity-conscious.

CHRISTIANITY VERSUS RELIGION

One of the best ways to put this coming and going in its right perspective is to consider seriously the true nature of

Christianity. When that is understood then a change in priorities more easily develops. Let's look at it with both eyes open.

Religion, by definition, is man's insatiable desire to discover God. Man has searched for God as long as there has been recorded history. That's why archaeologists have found hieroglyphics on the inside of caves representing divine figures. That's why Indians built totem poles. That's why, even in the remote tribes of the Amazon, idols and statues of a hundred gods have been found. Evidence abounds that people around the world have a desire to seek after at least some kind of god and know him and worship him.

However, Christianity is not in a technical sense a religion; for, I repeat, religion is man seeking God, but Christianity is God seeking man. Jesus in the flesh was God from heaven coming that great distance to earth "to seek and to save that which was lost" (Luke 19:10). Now, as it is the nature of Christianity that our God sought men, so it must be the nature of those who follow Christianity to seek men. We do not wait for men to come to our churches—that's religion. We go after them in the love of him who came from heaven on a seeking and saving mission.

Without question, many (maybe most!) churches are more religious than Christian. The people will *come,* but they won't *go.* They will come for religious activity, but they will not leave for Christian service. A witnessing course is announced and two hundred attend. Visitation is announced and twenty-five attend. Too many people who profess to be Christian would rather talk about doing something than do it.

Memorizing Scripture is a good thing to do. I recommend

it. But that is a religious activity. Doing in life what the Scripture you memorized said is the Christian application of that religious function. Singing songs is a good religious activity, but why sing lustily and religiously "Rescue the Perishing, Care for the Dying" when you leave not caring and never rescuing? That's called hypocrisy. Even listening to a sermon is no more than religious calisthenics if the truths of the message are not made a living daily part of the life of the hearer. To hear and do nothing, which is common, is religious busyness, but to hear and respond in disciplined regenerated living is Christian worship.

Frankly, many denominations have members galore who are superb at being religious and failures at being Christian. They forget that the group that hated Jesus Christ was the most religious group on earth. The members of that group faithfully attended their religious meetings, tithed, prayed loudly and eloquently, and helped crucify Jesus. Religion is still doing that today.

The nature of Christianity asks not, Why won't you come to my meeting? It asks instead, Why haven't I gone to my neighbor? Jesus came to us. We go to others. Oh, what a substitute religion becomes for getting involved in sharing Christ to a world hopeless apart from the Savior.

THE WORK OF THE CHURCH IS NOT AT CHURCH

After seeing that the nature of Christianity demands that we go to others as Jesus came to us, we can quickly see that church work is not exclusively or even primarily to be done at the church. The church is to meet at the building to receive the information and inspiration and leave eager to perform what it learned at the service. Going to the scheduled services is not performing our church work; it is learning how to perform it when we leave.

I knew of a school system in east Texas that consolidated with a larger system nearby. When this happened, it did away with the football team of the smaller school, but the cheerleaders still had their new uniforms, megaphones, and pompoms. They asked the principal of the school into which their school had been consolidated if they could have their own pep rallies on Thursday afternoons, since the regular pep rallies were on Friday. The principal approved. So, on Thursday afternoons the students of the consolidated school gathered in the auditorium and their cheerleaders onstage led them in the rousing cheers and fight songs of their old school. The problem was, they never played a game. In fact, they didn't even have a football team.

The church is to be the place where we have our pep rally to get excited about playing the game. Pep rallies may be thrilling and exciting, but if the game is never played, they are a mockery. Of course, they would soon lose their effectiveness when those in attendance realized it was just a lot of dead-end emotion. That's why hundreds of churches find it impossible to pump up the enthusiasm anymore. The people have seen the pep rallies, but somehow they never got out on the field of play where victory can be won. Soon even the pep rallies, called worship services at the church, lose their sense of validity.

I had a little fun one day teasing a lady at a church where I had just become pastor. She was giving me a tour of the facilities, pointing out their finer points. As we entered the beautiful auditorium she said to me, "Pastor, isn't our sanctuary gorgeous?" I replied, "Sanctuary, where are the ducks?" She, in astonishment, exclaimed, "Ducks, what do you mean, where are the ducks?" I said, "Well, a sanctuary is where you put ducks and other birds when you don't want them to be shot. The dictionary says that a sanctuary is 'an inviolable asylum.'" She said, "Oh, Pastor, you know what I mean." And I did. Regrettably, I knew.

Even though I admittedly made too much of the issue, I did it for a good purpose. The New Testament Christians knew nothing of a sanctuary that isolated them from the real world without their walls. They met in the gutters, sewers, and catacombs of Rome and left eager to shake the foundations of Caesar. They met for one purpose—to get equipped as soldiers to wage war against a world that was an enemy of the Cross. They didn't become a society of the satisfied, but rather they became a regiment of the ready and redeemed. As Wayne Dehoney said, "We are content to be the keepers of the aquarium, rather than fishers of men."

The word *auditorium* is really a better word than *sanctuary*. One seems to refer to a place to meet and then leave while the other implies a place to meet and then hide. Without exception, churches I've spoken at that talk of their "sanctuary" are far more difficult to stir toward revival than those who refer to their worship center as an "auditorium." No, I'm not a crusader for the word *auditorium*, but it is an issue that's deeper than mere semantics. It often reveals an attitude that believes the work of the church is done at the church, within the walls of that institution.

FATAL FELLOWSHIPS

One of the ways that a futile coming-and-going church attitude manifests itself is in what I call fatal fellowship. That is,
indeed, a subtle substitute for real evangelism, and its tribe
is increasing all the time. It is one of the more sinister substitutes because it has the appearance of congeniality,
warmth, love, and congregational compatibility.

What is fatal fellowship? A fatal fellowship is found in a
church body that majors on the sweet things of communion
with one another. Their songs are often about the church
being the family of God and how "we are one in the Spirit."
The melodies lend themselves to a schmaltzy sentimentalism
about the sacred tradition of days gone by. Sometimes the
fatal fellowship will even have a book display in the foyer of
the church with books written by everyone from a faith
healer to an ex-drug addict. And in conversation about the
array of books, the members will say that they have read
Cathy Coolgirl's (strictly anonymous) latest book, and it
"was just marvelous."

Sometimes the fatal fellowship will have dozens of grad-
uates of the latest seminar who carry their syllabus as loyally
as they carry their Bibles and read from both with equal
authority. There is now a fifth gospel, and they just happen
to have a copy of the inspired syllabus that they will be more
than happy to read from, especially when not asked to do so.
The *advanced* folks would not think of doing that, however—they'll just quote it by memory to you.

Everybody just loves everybody because they are all just
about alike. They have to be because it has been slightly promoted that they all go to the same training sessions. The fel-

lowship, they say, in this sacred society for snubbing sinners, is "just wonderful."

No, it's not wonderful. It stinks! Why? Because once again this mutual-admiration society has substituted its points and subpoints for a heartfelt burden for souls. They have comforted themselves with the idea that even though they are not seeing a lot of people saved, the Christians are getting some wonderful insights. And that is good. The church ought to do everything it can possibly do to help mature every Christian in the total truths of God's Word, but that must never become a substitute for winning people to a genuine conversion experience. When it does, it is a fatal fellowship that is guilty of spiritual murder by neglect.

One time I attended a church that had this sweet, syrupy fellowship of hugs and hallelujahs, precious thoughts, and "praise the Lord's." I was told they had baptized less than a dozen people the year before. I was there as a speaker for their Bible conference and when I got up to preach, the Lord impressed me to preach a message on being concerned for the lost, instead of the assigned subject. The message was not unordinarily good, I'm sure, but I preached it with a burdened heart. The Holy Spirit came upon that service and the people came in great numbers to say, "Oh, pray for me that I might stop just thinking of some new spiritual term I might learn, but that I might really get a vision for the lost people around me." Shortly after I left that city, the pastor called me and said, "Would you come back and preach a week on that? We've got to get busy for souls." I told him I would.

McGavran emphasizes that the best fellowship is from the overflow of evangelism. Says he,

One of the closest fellowships I ever saw in a church was in a men's group determined that it was going to reach its town for Christ. The members undertook a survey to determine need and then presented the gospel in many different ways of evangelism. In weekly meetings they reported on what had been done and then they planned and prayed for the future. In this meaningful work they had much good fellowship and came to know each other very intimately.[1]

Also hear Alvin Reid's word on this subject: "Do you want to build fellowship in your church? Then get a single-minded focus in the church—a focus on reaching people for Christ." Let me repeat, lest I be misunderstood—the sweet fellowship is good. The seminars are good and I have, personally, attended some of the better-known seminars and have benefited from them. The danger lies in the fact that too often one becomes spiritually fat on the sweet desserts of exciting new revelations while not sharing the main course with a hungry sinner. And when many like this get together in one church encouraging one another in their error, a fatal fellowship results.

True, biblical fellowship centers not on us but on the risen Christ. When a flood threatens a town, all the people come together in unity. They become close-knit in their sandbagging efforts. Why? They have a sense of urgency shared by all. We ought to build our fellowship in the fact that people are lost and we must bind together to win them.

The Christian experience is to be passed on. In a relay race where the baton is passed from one runner to the next, the runners who, having taken the baton, stop to polish it, sing a sentimental song about it, embrace it affectionately, or just admire it would never win. The baton must be quickly passed on.

That is exactly what we must do with the gospel—relay it to another who will relay it to another until glorious victory is won. Fellowships with that spirit will never be fatal, but they will be faithful. That, by the way, creates a fellowship that is genuinely warm and deeply permanent.

Too often fellowship is built around mutual mediocrity. All the people that really had a vision and desire to work have left. So, their fellowship is an unspoken but obvious agreement which is—we no longer have anybody making us feel guilty about being worthless. Yes, that will produce a sweet but fatal fellowship.

4

RESERVOIRS OF TRUTH OR RIVERS OF BLESSINGS?

Here is found one of the most subtle substitutes in Satan's arsenal of weapons. As I mentioned concerning the previous substitute, it, too, is particularly dangerous because it involves that which is very good. That, of course, is the heart of the problem—substituting good things for the best thing. This substitute is gaining in popularity, making it even more sinister. Its popularity is due to the fact that it more ably fits into our day of ease and affluence. Vital Christianity has few worse enemies than the "everything-made-easy" generation in which we find ourselves. Laziness has made its way not only down the streets of commerce but also among the pews of the parishioners. Thus the unspoken desire of many Christians is, I want to escape the strongest demands of witnessing if I can find another Christian function that relieves my guilt. God help us!

THE IDOLATRY OF THE BOOK

Every Christian should love the Bible, God's holy and infallible Word. It should always be a "lamp unto [our] feet, and a light unto [our] path" (Ps. 119:105). It contains 66 books, 1,189 chapters, and 33,102 verses, and every one of them is inspired from heaven itself. The older I become the more I appreciate this blessed Book and daily thank the Lord for supplying it in all of its richness. It is without peer, and sadly, there is too much ignorance of the Bible. One man said he was really concerned about our modern education. He said, "Could you believe my college freshman came home and asked me who Macbeth was? That's terrible. All he had to do was to look it up in the Bible." Yes, there is too much ignorance of the greatest of all books.

Everything, it seems, that man was born without he's been able to find a substitute for. Man couldn't fly through the air like the majestic eagle, so he made himself an airplane. And now, man can fly higher and faster than any bird God created. Man couldn't run across the earth like the tireless cougar, so he invented the automobile. Now, man can travel on earth faster than any creature. Man couldn't swim under the water like the various fishes of the sea, so he made himself a submarine and overcame that limitation. Man couldn't see in the darkness like the domestic cat, so he reached up into the sky and robbed it of its electricity; now in the blackest hour, man can flip a switch and darkness gives way to brilliant light.

You see, man has been able to find a better alternative for almost everything he innately didn't have, but there can never be an effective alternative for the Bible to meet the deepest needs of the human heart. For it is this Book that tells a man he is lost and the same Book that tells him how to be found everlastingly in Christ.

I love the story of the sophisticated Englishman who visited Brazil and approached a man of the Amazon region reading a Bible. The gentleman from London said, "Aha! In England we've outgrown that book." The former cannibal looked up into the ashen face of that man and said, "Sir, had we outgrown the Bible here, I would have eaten you yesterday." Indeed, there is power in God's Book!

All of the preceding is to let you know that I am a Bible man from the crown of my head to the tips of my toes. I believe every word in it. I defend it as God's inerrant Word, verbally inspired. Yet I must tell you that within itself, it is not to be worshiped, but it is to be an aid to worship. Some people have fallen down to worship the graven image they have made of the Bible and have never gotten up to do anything that the Bible tells them to do. My friend, if that is you, get up off your knees of idolatry and get on your feet of Christian service. God is not impressed with your kind and eloquent remarks concerning the Bible. It's going to stand without your rhetoric. God is impressed, however, when you take the teachings of his Word and use them to bring about spiritual revelation to your world. He's not looking for admiration for a book but obedience to his Word. Vance Havner had it right when he said you can be as straight as a gun barrel in your beliefs and be just as empty!

Far too many people have used the Bible as a medical student uses a cadaver. They examine it, dissect it, perform surgery on it, familiarize themselves with it, and learn its distinctive qualities. But as that future doctor cannot give life to a dead piece of humanity, so these people never get the Word alive in their life. They somehow fail to remember that the people who hated Jesus most were biblical scholars who had Scriptures over their doorposts, strapped to their bodies, and quoted chapters of it when their narrow-minded interpretation supported their warped views.

Saul of Tarsus once referred to himself as a "Jew among the Jews." He was an informed Hebrew, a Pharisee of the highest order, and greatly knowledgeable of the Old Testament, having been taught by the erudite Gamaliel. He was, besides being a biblical scholar, a murderer of Christians. That still exists in some forms today.

In one school that I attended, the girl who was known to be the easiest mark for indiscreet young men was the winner each year of the associational sword-drill contest. She could find Romans 12 faster than anyone, but she never presented her body "a living sacrifice, holy, acceptable unto God" (v. 1). She was the first to turn to Proverbs 31, but she was not a "virtuous woman" (v. 10) nor was she "a woman that feareth the LORD" (v. 30).

This extreme example profoundly illustrates the truth that one can know the Bible mechanically without knowing it spiritually. In fact, the reverse is true. He will live it, not just quote it. If one does know it spiritually, it will send him out, not set him down. It is soul-winning that makes one want to go to the Book and be obedient to all of its teachings. It is soul-winning that gives one a practical understanding of the Bible.

Roy J. Fish and J. E. Conant correlate this truth by saying,

The teaching received in Bible conferences and like places has meaning and value for the persistent soul-winners that it can have to no one else. Such a Christian will understand the deep truths of God and the Word that are not open to scholarship, but are understood through the Holy Spirit. The ever-active anointing of the Spirit which abides on the soul-winner makes the deep things plain and the great Doctrines luminous.[1]

It is inconceivable to me that people can study the Bible for years and not be winning others to Christ, for the Book they claim to know so well proclaims loud and clear on page after page that "he that winneth souls is wise" (Prov. 11:30). The truth of the matter is that it's much easier to sit among a few friends of the same socioeconomic group and dissect the Word than it is to get out on a hot day and grapple with the forces of hell seeking to win another to Christ. So a subtle substitute, once again, becomes a convenient escape from real evangelism.

There are churches that have made this idolatry the total personality of the church. These churches are occasionally large and have a tremendous interest in the Bible. Their pastors are men of the Book. Speakers of renown are brought in to lead conferences in deep study of biblical copies or books of the Bible. Almost always, those churches will have their own bookstore with all the aids for study by current big names in the field of biblical interpretation, prophecy, and so forth. The members leave the services and say on their way out, "Wasn't that rich? We were really fed." They are like a bakery that eats its own bread while a hungry world is ignored, but oh yes, they really do get fed.

Yet no invitation is given. Really though, why should there be? Conviction doesn't come by disassociated study of the Bible; it comes to open-hearted Christians who are always sensitive to the working of the Holy Spirit in their hearts through the burning application of the truth of God's Word. And, of course, another reason I suppose there is no need of an invitation is because very few if any lost people have been brought there by the well-informed members. They are about as well-informed or even more so about the Bible as Saul of Tarsus and often as dangerous!

Fed? Oh yes, they have been fed and fed and fed and fed. They are like the toad that got so full it couldn't hop. Someone once said to Dr. Alvin Reid, "We are looking for a church to get fed." His reply: "Why not take off your bib, put on an apron, and get to work for Jesus?"

When one of these churches was approached about its shortcomings in evangelism, one of the church leaders said, "Well, we feel that we've just got a different kind of ministry." He was certainly right—it's even different from a Christian ministry because a ministry for Christ has as its ultimate and primary concern the salvation of the lost. And one cannot rejoinder by saying, "Well, these conferences and studies help us to do that." No! They are conducted *instead* of doing that. Most of these people already know enough to win five worlds to Jesus, but they would prefer to boast of their learning. These good people need to understand that when they stand before God, he's not going to ask them to quote Psalm 115; he's going to ask, "Whom did you bring with you?"

Once again, Dr. Fish's updating of J. E. Conant's book *Every Member Evangelism* says it perfectly:

Today Bible conferences and conventions for the deepening of the spiritual life are proving to be a blessing to the whole church of Christ. But if the spiritual food received in them is not worked out in the normal activity of soul-winning, they may even prove to be a curse. Think of what is likely to result from a lot of suppressed sermons turned sour on our spiritual stomachs. No wonder fussy dyspeptics are ready to fight at a moment's notice over some nonessential doctrinal technicality. No wonder there are a few cranks, fanatics, and extremists abroad in the land. They are usually the kind who would walk a mile to a convention or a conference to hear some famous speaker, while they would hardly walk across the street to take Christ to a lost soul. They will pray with great fervency. "O Lord, give us a blessing," but they will mostly forget to pray, "O Lord, MAKE US a blessing."[2]

Those who have made an idol of the Bible have become reservoirs of truth instead of blessings. Someone may say, "Well, you've got to know something before you can share it." True! But knowing does not preclude sharing, especially when the knowing becomes a substitute for the real work of the Christian soldier, which is to present the gospel to those who are unsaved.

It is more than coincidental that years before Germany began to go insane under Nazism, the leading Protestant denomination there lost its evangelistic zeal and churches became introverted sanctuaries of sacred studies. Their churches lost their militant commitment to winning their country for Christ; when Hitler's swastikas began to blight every city and village, far too many Christians joined the

ranks of the new movement. Yes, some died for their faith—
men like Dietrich Bonhoeffer who believed in propagating
the gospel and paying the full price of discipleship.

England, years ago, decided just to have conferences and
Bible studies. Even their Sunday school became a place of
Bible study apart from outreach. Yes, they learned the Bible
and now only 2 percent of the people in England attend
church.

I recommend that we study the Bible as never before,
memorize it, and cherish it with the deepest feelings of our
hearts. Then (and there must be a *then*) we should take what
we've learned and share blessed Jesus with the rich and the
poor, the handsome and the ugly, the longhairs, the short-
hairs, and the nohairs and let our world know that we are
not trying to be only students of the Word, but also soldiers
of the cross.

THE TECHNO AGE

I'll not spend much time here, but because of the current
craze for technology, it is at least worth a mention. Not only
has reading become a substitute for evangelism but listening
to various and sundry CDs, radio programs, and television
shows has also become a substitute. At first only a few
people were involved, but now thousands of Christians have
found their refuge from demanding soul-winning behind
their CD players. Once again, the result is reservoirs of truth
instead of rivers of blessings.

Let me be quick to say that I'm grateful for the availability of good recorded messages. Recorded messages have min-
istered to the sick, shut-ins, and hundreds in remote areas and

by and large have been a rich blessing to many, including this writer. In fact, my own church has an extensive CD ministry and sends out several hundred CDs a month.

The problem, however, is the same. For those who shy away from being personal evangelists, this provides another haven where they can feel good by doing something Christian but at the same time neglect their essential responsibility. In the past ten years, hundreds of new fads have had spectacular popularity because they offer a seemingly legitimate excuse for not evangelizing.

I'm thinking of a middle-aged lady that I once knew. She had recorded messages by everybody that I had ever heard of and recorded messages by many I hadn't heard of. Her investment in equipment and CDs had to total several thousand dollars. She thought I was backslidden, for at that time I wasn't listening to CDs. She would bring me CDs and tell me that I just had to hear Brother W.; he was "just wonderful." Occasionally, she was right and the sermon was excellent. She even had a CD club that met at her house once a week to listen to and exchange CDs. But for the five years I knew her and her friends in the CD club, they never, even collectively, led one person—I'm telling you, not one person—to Christ. Everything went into the ear and came out nowhere. Oh, how effective the devil's substitutes are! Sermons can be found online, but sinners are found by going to share.

Cases just like this are prominent across the country. One such CD club met one evening a week, but not a single member of that CD club attended church visitation. They preferred hearing about it and doing nothing about it. Stagnant reservoirs instead of refreshing rivers.

Another problem inherent in the present craze over CDs

is that often the medium is confused for the message. That is, some feel if it's a CD by a Christian, it has to be good and doctrinally sound, especially if it was given to them by a spiritual-talking friend. My brother-in-law went to a Baptist church a couple of years ago to conduct a revival meeting. He noticed in the church's huge library CDs by scores of people who were greatly opposed to basic Baptist teaching and practice. He said the services were noticeably lacking in spiritual power and evangelistic results, and he understood why when he saw this display of heretical and cultic tapes. The members had been filling their minds with garbage and didn't even know they were spiritually underfed. Some of the members thought if it was on CD it just had to be good. The medium became the message.

It isn't true that by listening to CDs, even good CDs, one will grow in the Lord and be doctrinally sound. Even tapes on witnessing and sharing the faith must never become substitutes for doing it. It is true, however, that consistent soul-winning will lead one to have a great desire to know the sound doctrines of God's Word.

"Doctrinal troubles and questions about the Word of God are seldom raised," say Fish and Conant, "by active soul-winners. The fundamentals of the faith are in no danger among those who are persistently seeking the lost. Heresy cannot live in an atmosphere created by spiritual health."[3] Also, soul-winners are usually the ones growing most rapidly in their faith. Win Arn observed,

> I've discovered that those who have found Christ and who actively participate in finding others are actually growing in grace. They are being perfected. They are sharing the

mind of Christ more than Christians who never search for
the lost. In other words, if Christians are involved in meaningful outreach, they themselves are going to grow better,
faster and more effectively as Christians.[4]

I'll have more to say later about the substitute of radio
and television. Christian radio stations are everywhere now.
In fact, many Christians enjoy listening to so many Christian
programs that they don't have time to do anything Christian.
Many of the faithful watchers and listeners have become
superficial blobs of joy and nothing more. They say "praise
the Lord" with their lips and "go to hell" with their lives.

FROM FOLDING CHAIR TO PEW TO GRAVE

Human reservoirs are found all over the church; they are
people into whom has flowed a wealth of teaching and
preaching. Through the years they have sat in a Sunday
school class soaking in the study of the Bible; they have
heard the exposition of Scripture from the pulpit; and outside of giving a little money, they have done little else. Their
Christian life could be outlined something like this: They sit
in a folding chair in Sunday school, the pew at church, and
they lie down in their final (there were several previous resting places) resting place, the grave.

There are churches with several hundred members who
began at church as children and lived many decades more as
members of the same church before their funeral was conducted there, and they had done nothing more than transfer
dead weight from the folding chair of Sunday school to the
pew of the auditorium. They faithfully (thank the Lord for

faithful members!) repeated this process year after year after year but never once directed a department, taught a class, made a visit, brought a visitor, or won a person to our Lord. They had heard enough spiritual truths to melt the Iron Curtain but had not even gotten their neighborhood warm for Jesus—reservoirs of truth instead of rivers of blessings.

Shouldn't there be a time when people graduate from the class of learning into the world of service? Shouldn't people who sit in various Sunday school classes for ten to forty years and never take the truths they have learned to be blessings to a blighted world be ashamed of their idleness? Maybe these people should be taken out of their cozy beds of inactivity and assigned twenty names of lost people who have somehow gotten on the roll but never come. Why not tell them they are through in the Esther Class, for it's time they graduated and got busy reaching people for Christ. Surely only a very few adults should spend more than ten years just being a student in Sunday school. There ought to come a day when the student either becomes a teacher, an outreach leader, or a director.

Frankly, far too many of our Sunday school classes have become for "me and Dorah and no morah." Many of them have become clubs where visitors are made to feel uncomfortable because they are interfering with the classes' plans to remain stagnant. After all, how can you be concerned about visitors and prospects and plan the monthly potluck dinner for the "faithful ones" in the class?

Am I overstating the case? I think not. This is a factual evaluation of thousands of Christians in churches across America. They sit and listen so they can leave and come back and sit and listen, so they can leave and . . .

Charles McKay is right:

The Sunday School is the greatest evangelistic agency of a church. It assures permanency in evangelism. The pastor who realizes his opportunity through the Sunday School and rightfully uses it, is wise indeed. The program of Christian Education in any church, if not geared to evangelism, will prove to be a hindrance. Every agency of a church should contribute to the evangelistic endeavor of that church. One that does not, has no right to exist. It is, or should be, all for evangelism.[5]

What is the answer? People in our churches must be made to see that church is not where we come to do the work of Christ but rather where we come to learn how to do the work of Christ. Church leaders must focus in on the individual, uncover his buried potential, and motivate him to aggressively get involved in reaching people for Christ. This can be done by either assigning the person so many people by name to reach or by showing him how he could take a survey of just the block he lives on and not rest until that whole block is saved and in Sunday school growing in Christian maturity.

The problem is that the church staff is often satisfied with reaching a certain numerical goal and forgets the gigantic numbers that could be reached if more people were involved. Somehow we in leadership must get our people, all of them who are physically and emotionally able, out of the classrooms, off of the pews, and into the homes and hearts of the millions outside of Christ. Christianity is vastly more than years of warming a folding chair and occupying a pew.

5

CULTIVATION DURING HARVEST TIME

Satan often treats the Christian the same way he treats a lost person. That is, he rarely tells a lost person not to accept Christ as his or her Savior; he usually just says "Not now." And so a lifetime of "not now's" are strung together until that person spends eternity apart from Christ. He very seldom tells the Christian not to share his or her faith because the devil knows that most Christians at least give intellectual assent to the fact that the Bible teaches witnessing. He just says, "Not now."

Therefore, untold numbers of Christians go through life plowing and cultivating their lost friends but never deeply planting the seed of conviction into the soil of their souls and harvesting those lives for the Master. How does this subtle substitute usually raise its head?

WIN THEIR RESPECT

A popular thought often entertained by the timid witness is that in order to lead a person to Christ, you must, over a period of months or sometimes years, do things that will win respect. In many cases a person can only be reached in this way. I've seen this in my own soul-winning experiences. But, it's not always the case, so concerned witnesses must be open to the many times they need to witness at the first encounter. Neither Jesus nor the apostle Paul was bashful about sharing the good news at every opportunity. I'm certain that there are millions in hell today who wish the Christians hadn't delayed in telling them how to be saved. There is no need to be rude or obnoxious, but at least find out if this person you've just come in contact with knows Christ and if not offer a brief presentation of the gospel. You might be the only person who ever witnessed to that person and you may never see him or her again.

One time I was leading a revival in one of our southern states, and the pastor and I stopped at a filling station for some gas. The owner of the station was seated inside while one of his employees waited on us. I went inside and began to witness to this man, and he followed every word with his eyes as I read from my New Testament. Never have I seen a man more interested in what the Bible had to say about his need of God. In just a few moments the pastor rushed into the station and, seeing what I was doing, blustered out, "Hey, Joe (not the real name of this owner), the university really has a team this year, doesn't it?" Joe said, "Sure do." Then he put his index finger on a page of the Testament, preparing to ask me a question, when once again the pastor interrupted, "Well, come on now, Bailey, we've got to get to this lady's house; she'll never forgive us if dinner gets cold." The pastor pulled me by the arm and we left. As we got in the car he said to me, "Man, you were about to mess everything up. I want to win his respect before I witness to him." I said, "How long have you been trying to do this?" He sheepishly said, "Well, about six years."

Three nights after that stop at the filling station, Joe lay dead of a heart attack at age forty-three. My heart breaks to think where Joe is today.

This was even more vividly brought to my mind several years before that incident. I was working for a construction company building houses in Dallas, Texas. One young man I worked with—we'll call him Tom—was obviously lost. He was a handsome young man of nineteen, who had been married only a few months. He knew that I would be on my way to a Baptist college in the fall to be a ministerial student. I lived a good example before him those two months of June and July, refusing to listen to the filthy jokes and never participating in the cursing and beer drinking.

The last week of July, my dad and I came in from church and my mother, who was ill and had remained home that day, handed me a copy of the *Dallas Times Herald* and began to cry. A small article told about Tom drowning Saturday afternoon in Lake Texhoma. Then I remembered back to Friday afternoon when he told me that he and our boss were going fishing. I went to my room terribly depressed, realizing that for two months I had worked side by side with this lost young man and had never even given him a chance to say no! I kept telling myself that I needed to win his respect and develop a friendship. What I really needed to do was to win his soul and the Holy Spirit would develop a friendship.

It still hurts to this hour to realize that at least one person, for sure, will be eternally lost because of the silent lips of Bailey Smith. Maybe that's what the Bible means when it talks of "weeping and wailing, and gnashing of teeth." Some on that final day will weep and wail because we never told them how to receive the gift of eternal life.

I would not encourage anyone to be crass and boisterous and disrespectful in the sharing of faith, but I would encourage all of us to be more alert to the daily opportunities we have to share our testimony with new acquaintances in the sweet spirit of Jesus. The other day I listed sixty-one names of active, loyal, maturing, tithing, witnessing, and joyful Christians in our church who were recently saved after knowing the person who witnessed to them less than an hour.

C. E. Autrey, one of the greatest authorities on evangelism in the world, says, "Every experienced soul-winner has seen men, women, and children make decisions for Christ the very first time they were ever approached on the matter. These decisions were genuine and the life lived afterwards proved it."[1]

If the witness is shared and the person rejects, don't bitterly rebuke him or her. Have prayer and thank the Lord for the person's kindness in listening to you. Then, from the moment after the sharing, begin if possible to win that person's respect and develop that friendship until another and better opportunity presents itself to share Jesus. Some people I've been able to win in ten minutes, but for others it might take several years. Just don't allow "winning their respect" to become a cop-out for you.

Several years ago our ministry conducted an areawide crusade in Laurel, Mississippi, with forty-one churches participating. It was a grand and glorious week of hundreds of people being saved and other lives being turned around for the cause of Christ.

I discovered that the person most committed to the week was a man by the name of Richard Headrick, a local businessman. He was involved through his attendance and through his finances. No one gave more that week than Mr. Headrick. It seemed that he and I became instant friends. But I felt in my heart that he did not truly know the Lord. Although I knew he was an active member of a local Baptist church, I just did not sense that he had a walk with Christ.

Early one Thursday morning he called me and came to my room at a local motel. We fellowshipped for quite a while as he indicated to me that he had had many sleepless nights thinking about some of the things I had said in my messages. It wasn't long until we were both on our knees and Richard Headrick prayed the sinner's prayer. However, I later learned that he was not really saved at that point.

Sometime after that a deacon in a Baptist church in the city of Laurel was saved during our crusade even though he had been involved in church work all of his life. He had been on several executive committees of denominational boards and agencies. He was chairman of the finance committee at his church and a Bible teacher but still was not saved. In fact, he said to me after the crusade that his pastors had protected him from heaven. I thought that was a strong statement. I understood what he was trying to say. He was trying to say, in essence, that because he was a successful man, a man known for being financially able, a man involved in denominational programs, preachers might be afraid to approach him as firmly as he needed to be approached.

However, one night when I was preaching on the subject of Judas Iscariot, this man to whom I have been referring, Sid Hughes, walked the aisle and gave his life to Christ. He said that he would set his alarm every night to wake up at 3:00 A.M. and sit on the side of the bed and thank Jesus for that night he was genuinely born again.

Well, it was this man, Sid Hughes, who got Richard Headrick in his car sometime later and would not let him wiggle out of the fact that he was really lost. Mr. Headrick told me that Sid verbally pounded and pounded him to the point of irritation. It was that relentless confrontation that let Richard Headrick see he had not really been saved. It is really this encounter with Jesus in the car with Sid Hughes that Richard points to as his salvation.

Richard and his precious wife, Gina, recently sold their business for millions of dollars and have become very generous benefactors to many Christian causes. All of that may have never happened had it not been for the strong preaching of the gospel and the faithful witness of a godly layman who got saved after being in church all of his life.

The point is well made—some men are only won to Christ by strong, persistent, relentless confrontation. I've long discovered that strong people must be witnessed to by another strong person with a strong presentation. Strong people like Mr. Headrick can see through plastic and anything not real. May God give us strong, powerful witnesses for Jesus. Unless that happens some potentially bold people and potentially wealthy people who could help the cause of Christ may never be reached.

THE WRONG WAY VERSUS NO WAY

You've probably heard of the person who criticized the soul-winner by saying, "I don't like the way you witness." The soul-winner replied, "How do you do it?" The critic said, "I don't." The soul-winner said, "Well, I like my method better!"

It has become popular to criticize the person with a strong desire to win souls. Yes, I'm aware that many people have made mistakes in sharing their faith, but we cannot allow mistakes and excuses of others to excuse our callous indifference. There are thousands of parents who have made mistakes rearing children, but I'm certainly grateful that my wife and I didn't let that stop us from having our three sons. God does not allow us to hide behind other people's faults to pardon our poor witnessing. It's not other people's errors that keep us from witnessing; it's our own lack of commitment. Bill Bright is right when he says the only failure in witnessing is the failure to witness.

Time after time, I've listened in churches, youth fellowships, and retreats to folks sarcastically bemoaning those who have a genuine burden for souls. Many times I've heard various speakers say, "Now don't go out to get a person saved so you can put another notch on your gun barrel." Why not? Wouldn't it be super if all Christians in the world would set numerical goals for their soul-winning? Wouldn't it be great if the deacons in all our churches would set a goal of winning at least one person a month to Christ who walks the aisle of the church, gets baptized, and becomes involved in Bible study and training? God, give us a million Christian marksmen who have their witnessing guns completely covered with notches representing those who have been saved through their love for them.

I know we shouldn't witness like salesmen looking for customers, because in doing so we too often only talk the "sales pitch," neglecting to listen to the people's distinctive needs and inner longings. It's true that we don't want to get a yes from them that is meaningless, just to get our quota. But most of the critics who warn us of these extremes create a false option. It is not a choice between high-pressure salesmanship and nothing. There is a right way of carrying on an aggressive soul-winning practice with numerical goals in mind. Essentially, that is done by keeping the heart right through daily prayer and submission to the Holy Spirit, asking God to help you to always have the right motive as you go. Then go with a heart ablaze for the lost souls, seeking to win all that will come to the Savior.

How about this matter of salesmanship? It is usually bad when applied to soul-winning, but listen to the other side of the story. Often the devil has the lost person so entangled in the affairs of this life that it is not easy for him or her to understand the gospel or to let go of the old life. When that person is witnessed to, Satan immediately begins to whisper everything he can into that person's mind and heart. All the demons of hell attack that person, wanting to keep him or her in their clutches. Consequently, there may have to be much time spent in Scripture reading, prayer, and persuasion to get that person to see the need for God. Yes, even persuasion. There is nothing wrong with persuasion that is properly and prayerfully motivated because at the moment of that witnessing experience, all of the forces of darkness are trying to persuade that lost person to stay lost.

I was sharing Christ with a man in New Mexico on one occasion. The presence of Satan was powerful that Sunday afternoon, as was the presence of God. My deacon friend and I read to that dear man, prayed for him, and tried to persuade him to turn from wrong to right. He would almost break, but then he would stiffen again and go back toward the devil. I really felt that God was going to save him that day, so after almost two hours I said, "Sir, you can be saved if you will just pray and ask God to forgive you of your sins and invite Christ into your life. Let's kneel and pray. Go ahead." The dear deacon and I got down on our knees and for over twenty minutes there was stone silence. Then the old man began to groan and sob and finally in a triumphant release of victory, he shouted, "Dear God, save me, forgive me; I don't want the devil's way anymore." Oh, what a victory it was for that man and for his family.

This is what I'm saying. It's not so much salesmanship as it is that often a price has to be paid to win a soul to Christ. Quick tricks won't do it. Caring is always costly. Soul-winning is work. That's why so many have looked for and found a substitute. Commitment is the answer. Commitment means willingness to take the plunge, to assure the risk, to leave the bridges behind us, to throw everything we have and are into the cause to which we have committed ourselves. And it must be a commitment to harvest.

There is a story worth repeating that illustrates this point. A fearful storm had ruined a splendid crop of grain. Other crops all about had been gathered before the storm struck, but this one could not be harvested for lack of help.

The owner of the crop stood at the fence after the storm had passed, looking at his ruined harvest, his face a picture of sadness and dejection.

A stranger walking along the road came up to the fence and stood in silence for a moment beside the farmer. Then he said, "It's a pretty sad sight, isn't it?"

"You would really think it was sad if it were your field. I couldn't get any harvesters," was the owner's sad reply as he turned on his heel and went to the house.

While we are begging the Lord to send the sheaves in to be gathered, a ripened harvest is going to eternal waste because the laborers are not going out into the field to gather it in.

Much wrong has been done in regard to witnessing, and the worst is no witnessing at all. Cultivation must lead to at least attempted harvest or the cultivation is wasted mockery. Cultivation is a substitute for evangelism when there is no sincere intention for the cultivation to lead to harvest.

DON'T BOTHER THEM

Satan is very effective with this devious tool. He tells us that it's all right to befriend a lost soul and win his respect, but to not ever give him a strong witness because that could offend him and bother him. Thus a good opportunity occurs and we open our mouths to set up the witnessing interview when the voice to the heart comes: "Oh, there will be another time; don't disturb him." I wonder how many people are in hell because of the Christians who have been afraid they might disturb somebody.

One time in Colt, Arkansas, a pastor and I were out

soul-winning, and as we came to the house of the man we were so concerned for, we saw he was painting his house. It was a hot, sultry August day. The thought came to both of us, *Let's not disturb that man while he's working.* But we did stop and begin witnessing to the man. He was a little huffy and resistant at first as he wiped the perspiration and paint from his face. Soon, however, he had invited Jesus into his heart, and that night at the revival service he publicly made his profession of faith. The church resounded with rejoicing because that man had been prayed for, for many years.

The next summer, I went back for a revival and, as I pulled into the parking lot of the church, that man had his hand on the door handle of my car before I could turn off the motor. He opened my door and fell on my neck saying, "Preacher, thank you for interrupting my painting last summer. This has been the best year of my life for me and my family."

People, indeed, are complacent. Only Jesus can rightly shake them out of that lethargy. Remember, it is the being awakened that allows one to escape at night from the burning house. Sleep leads to death.

One of the finest deacons of our church came to me after a recent service and very emotionally asked to talk with me. We got over in a corner and he told me how a few months back God had told him to share Christ with his boss that particular day, but he didn't do it. He said, "Something kept telling me not to bother my busy boss." On the following weekend that boss and his girlfriend were killed by lightning as they spent the night together in a cabin by a lake. He said, "Pastor, during the invitation I heard my boss saying from hell, 'Why didn't somebody tell me? Why didn't somebody tell me!'"

Alvin Reid tells his students, "Lost people are more amazed at our silence than offended at our message." We must tell them the good news!

Listen, dear reader, now is the time for harvest. You will do lots of planting and sowing and cultivating just through consistent witnessing. Today is the day of salvation. Quickly share redemption's story with friends, relatives, and all those apart from Christ. It's better to give them a chance to say yes than to remain silent and never know what their response might have been.

6

THEORETICAL
EARNESTNESS WITHOUT
COMMITTED WORK

The title will be explained as the chapter unfolds, but just let me say this much to begin. There is a tendency to believe that one's words are the same as acting upon the words. This is much like when your mother got you to eat all your spinach because of the starving children in China. How that helped the Chinese children you were never sure, but it made Mom feel better in her heart to talk about it even though she had no plan to alleviate their hunger. Words often become substitutes for performing the actions indicated in the words—a verbal treadmill that goes nowhere, if you please. This is especially true in the area of evangelism. Let's look at how this theoretical earnestness without commitment expresses itself.

COURSES WITHOUT CAUSES

Throughout the world of Christianity, there is a prevalent desire to take and to teach courses. This is undeniably good. All Christians should be concerned about learning all they can in order to be better-informed people. There are courses being taught in churches and at denominational functions on everything from submissive womanhood to karate. There is a popular trend of daytime Bible studies that draw huge crowds of ladies. All serious-minded Christians are grateful for this interest in learning. Thousands of people have been helped by this emphasis.

Where is the problem then? you ask. The problem is that far too often the courses become ends within themselves— obviously not for everyone, but for many. For instance, there are thousands of ladies I've known who have taken every mission course ever offered, but they have never themselves become missionaries. Many of them will pass in their automobiles fifty mission opportunities on their way to be a part of a mission study. Will they ever stop and meet the needs of those fifty mission opportunities? Probably not! Why? Because they feel that in talking earnestly about the theory of missions, they have shown mission concern and forget their personal responsibility to get their hands dirty in the real world of mission action. I know of a lady who has enough study course certificates to paper every room of her house, but she refuses to take one card with a lost person's name on it. She is a professional study course taker and teacher. She is guilty of the rankest hypocrisy.

I once rode in a car with a group of people on my way to speak at a Real Evangelism Conference. We had all been out to eat at a very lovely restaurant in that sprawling and beautiful southern city. As we drove along, moving our toothpicks to each needed area of our mouths, we meandered through one very poor and racially divergent neighborhood. I felt strange inside as I looked at the little children playing in cramped apartment yards, old people sitting on hard, hot concrete steps, mothers hanging out clothes with babies strapped to their backs and toddlers wrapped around their ankles, and men with jackhammers and picks on the streets earning their bread by the sweat of their brow. I said a little prayer to myself, "God forgive me for my professionalism. Don't let me just be involved in talking evangelism; encourage me to be involved in evangelism itself. I want to love these people I see right now and tell them about Jesus." We didn't stop, however, because we didn't want to be late for our evangelism seminars.

Sometimes the church looks to the world like a luxury liner going through the ocean with drowning people all around it. Some are going down for the first time, others for the second time, and still others for the last time. The drowning people look up at the luxury liner (the church) and yell, "Help us! Help us; we're drowning; save us." But the voice comes back from the ship, "Oh, be quiet, we're trying to take a study course on how to be concerned for drowning people." That's what I call theoretical earnestness without committed work.

After I preached at one state Evangelism Conference, a very emotional lady took me by the arm and said she just had to talk with me. We found an unoccupied Sunday school room, and after seating ourselves in chairs made for small children, she began to open her heart to me. "Keep this confidential, please," she said. "I'm employed by my denomination, and I've gone all over this state and many places across America teaching courses on missions. People always tell me what a good job I do." Her conversation was interrupted by sobs of conviction. "But I've got to tell you tonight, Bailey, that I have never won an adult person to Christ in all of my life. I feel like a professional fake."

I tried to tell her she was being too hard on herself and gave her some words of encouragement about her personal evangelism. We had prayer and went our respective ways. Three months later, in another state, this same lady ran up to me after I had preached and began hitting me on both shoulders with the palms of her hands saying, "I did it. I did it. I did it." I knew what she meant, but jokingly I said, "What did you did?" She said, "Ten days after we last talked, I led a young husband and his wife to Christ, and they came and were baptized and joined our church. I've got some more on the string now, and I've never been happier in my life. I'm still teaching courses on missions, but the difference is I'm a missionary too."

She realized that courses without causes are curses and that missions is not where you are but what you're doing. It is blatant hypocrisy to appear concerned about people in Upper Volta, Africa, when we don't have enough genuine love to stop our car at the little neighborhood house and share our faith in Christ—theoretical earnestness without committed work.

McGavran says, "Many leaders, both laymen and ministers, get tied to programs which have little to do with the propagation of the Gospel and nothing to do with finding the lost. A minister can get trapped in splendid work whether the church grows or not."[1] God help us not to do that.

What a great day it is to see that many of our seminaries, as a part of their evangelism classes, actually go out to witness. At one seminary, at least two weeks of the required personal evangelism class is given to actual soul-winning activity. In one class, forty-three people were saved through the witness of these students.

SPEECHES THE SPEAKERS FORGET

Time and again speeches have been made about sacrifice, but the speaker didn't plan to make a personal sacrifice. Speeches have been made on love, and the speaker is rude to the waitress at the local café afterward. Speeches have been made on the absolute necessity of fair play and thoughtfulness, yet the next day, the speaker pays the lady who helps his wife around the house only five dollars for her day's labor. Another speaker might roll up rhetorical tidal waves as he pleads for Christian ethics in our modern society, then drive seventy miles per hour going home after the service. A pastor addresses his young people and tells them it is imperative that they always be honest at school. "Cheating is out for a Christian," he says. "Always respect your teachers and school administrators, for the Bible teaches submission to authority," he continues. Then while driving to the associational meeting the following day, he will utilize his radar detector.

I have often wondered if speeches are for speaking purposes only. Maybe we need to tell the audience before we start that we worked hard on the message we have for them but to not take it too seriously. Have the speakers and preachers told their listeners by their own lives that there is no connection between what is said and what is to be done? Many times I've heard messages where several illustrations were given about the sacrifices made on the mission field. The listeners weep when they hear that some Christian farm laborer might give years of savings that he had held back to purchase the only car of his life to help build the little mission building. The speaker's voice breaks in emotion. The congregation sobs, but few go home, including the preacher, and offer their life savings to God.

Is it that we have come to accept the fact that speeches are intended to move our emotions but not our lives? Have we accepted the idea that illustrations are to be given because they are interesting, but "don't expect me to identify with that story." Is there a contest to see who can give the most dramatic and touching sermon for which the audience can mentally award an A+, but as far as letting the message change their life style, or the preacher's for that matter, they say, "Let's forget it"?

My wife judges a television movie by the number of facial tissues she uses during the viewing to wipe her eyes. One-tissue movies are fair, but if it's a three-tissue movie, it's a knockout. Could we be that way about sermons? If the sermon makes us cry, laugh, or if we were impressed with sentence structure, it was good.

No! No! No! Sermons are not to be sermon-centered; they are to be people-centered. They are good not when they make you laugh or cry but when they cause you to change your life. A good sermon helps change sinners to saints, prostitutes to virtuous ladies, dope addicts to ministers, unfaithful church members to pillars of the church, haters to lovers, gossips to kind speakers, silent Christians to bold witnesses, and the apathetic to disciples electric with the spirit of Jesus.

This attitude greatly affects the area of reaching people for Christ. Preacher and deacon alike will give scores of devotionals on the condition of a lost world, then fail to make bold decisions in the church that might reach the lost world. A deacon may speak before the deacons meeting begins on the terrible problems of juvenile delinquency and then vote against the church outreach program for youth because it costs too much money.

One pastor told me of one of his men who cried "crocodile tears" when he talked of the plight of little children in the neighborhood for whom no one cared. However, when the church wanted to start a bus ministry, he said he was against it because "the kind of kids you pick up on buses would mistreat the church property." That's what is called theoretical earnestness without committed work. Our churches are full of that type of empty concern, and the tragedy is that those people with the theoretical earnestness think they are genuinely interested in the things of God. But they are not really interested until their lives are involved in their commitment. I read a little quote on a wall plaque that is so true it hurts: "I practice daily what I believe. Everything else is religious talk."

PARALYSIS OF POWERLESS PRAYING

Very few things are so pitifully lacking in modern Christian living as a consistent prayer life. The Father so wants us to fellowship and commune with him through prayer. It is true that the "effectual fervent prayer of a righteous man availeth much," yet we have become a people of hard hearts and soft knees.

Harold Lindsell, speaking to the United States Congress of Evangelism meeting in Minneapolis, Minnesota, said concerning prayer, "You and I are called upon to communicate the Gospel to evangelize the world, and all of the power that we need for this can be found in prayer, and in the Spirit, and in love. These are the instruments which are ours, for the weapons of our warfare are not carnal. If you look to education, you get what education can do. If you look to eloquence, you get what eloquence can do. If you look to armies, you get what armies can do. If you look to diplomacy, you get what diplomacy can do. But if you look to prayer, you get what God can do."[2]

Yes, I definitely believe in the power of prayer. When we lived in Hobbs, New Mexico, my wife became very sick. She had a high fever for thirty-four days. One day her doctor called me to his office and in a very serious moment told me that they had seen a "suspicious spot on her liver" and all six x-rays had confirmed its existence. He told me they would do exploratory surgery the next morning.

I was sick at heart and drove home with tears flowing down my face. I called Roswell, New Mexico, and canceled a speaking engagement because Dr. McCormick had told me to be in Sandy's hospital room when he told her of the surgery. I then called my father-in-law, who is a genuine man of God and told him what the doctor had said about his daughter. At the time he was in Arkansas with more than one hundred preachers at a retreat site. He shared this with all of those preachers and they began to pray. Many of them called their churches to ask their people to pray. Of course, I prayed with our little sons for hours.

That night I was in the room with my wife, greatly concerned how she would take the news. Every time I looked at her I choked up and had to hide my emotions from her. After what seemed to be an eternity, Dr. McCormick walked in and without saying hello, said, "Well, how would you like to go home in the morning?" I thought that he surely wasn't playing some kind of cruel game. No, the arrangements were made for her release.

I followed the doctor out into the hall and said, "Doc, what's the deal? You told me to be here tonight because you were going to break the news to her about surgery. What's going on?" He said, "Pastor, everything has been done for her operation. The surgical room is reserved and the time for the operation is on the hospital schedule. But this afternoon we took some more x-rays just to locate the best place for the incision and there was no spot on her liver." He continued, "We turned her to several different positions and took more pictures and she is as normal as I am. You can take your wife home in the morning."

Oh, people, I can't tell you what I felt. When that good doctor left me, I leaned my face against the wall of the hospital corridor and cried like a baby. Among many other expressions of gratitude, I said, "Thank you, God, for the power of prayer that sent the Great Physician to do his work making the other work unnecessary."

Yes, I know God doesn't always choose to heal. I also know he does choose to heal. I will always believe it was God's sovereign merciful care in response to hundreds and maybe thousands of prayers that brought healing to my beautiful wife.

Allow me to relate just one more dramatic answer to prayer. Many great answers that are not dramatic come to prayer, but I want to share this one to let each reader know for sure that I believe in the power of prayer. In one of my pastorates I was sick and had a need for a supply preacher for our Sunday services. I contacted a young preacher who agreed to preach for me, but I was later informed that because of unique circumstances, it might be better if he didn't. I considered on this particular Saturday night whether to call and explain to him the situation and ask him not to preach. I decided, however, that that would not be ethical, so I didn't call. I did pray, "Lord, the matter is in your hands. If it's best for him not to preach, you will have to do something about it."

The young man was to preach twice on Sunday morning, once at the early service and then at the eleven o'clock service. Ten minutes into his message at the early service his jaw was painfully locked open and he could not speak. He was rushed to the emergency room of a hospital because of the excruciating pain. He, of course, could not preach the eleven o'clock service either. That had never happened to him before nor has it since. He probably wishes I had made that call on Saturday night.

God does hear and answer prayer. We never stand higher than when we're kneeling. Head bowed, eyes closed is the position for clearest vision.

I have indicated how vitally important prayer is, but prayer is powerless when it becomes a substitute for evangelism. Evangelism is a task. It is doing something. Just as

God did not save humanity by merely making a decree from heaven, but rather his Son suffered and died, neither can we win our world to Christ by just praying. Pray we must, but prayer for the lost without going to the lost is insincere concern—if concern at all. Prayer is to be an aid to action, not a substitute for sharing. It is true that prayer puts spiritual powers in motion, but God has chosen us to reap the harvest of prayers. Thousands of people in our cities are prayed for by friends or maybe even by a mother hundreds of miles away, which has made those persons prepared prospects for Christ, but they are not saved because no one has faced them with the claims of our Lord. These prospects don't need further prayer; they need the witness of a person whose heart is ablaze for the souls of people.

Where is prayer most effective in reaching the lost? It is not prayer for the lost, even though I have already stated our need for that. The most effective praying is not for the lost world but rather for the saved to have a concern for the world that's lost. Remember, Jesus had to do something in order to provide a way of salvation, and it is true today that Jesus' followers must do more than pray; they must go and witness.

Did Jesus ever tell his disciples to pray that the unsaved would begin following him? Of course not. He did say, however, "Pray ye therefore the Lord of the harvest, that he will *send forth labourers* into his harvest" (Matt. 9:38, italics added). Prayer, then, is to be used to awaken the saved to the lostness of the lost. Most people who are honestly, genuinely sought for Jesus are reached for salvation and Christian service. Do you doubt that? I challenge you to prove otherwise. It is true. I repeat, most people who are

85

prayerfully, conscientiously witnessed to by a sincere soul-winner do give their hearts to Christ. The problem then is not the world's lack of interest in Jesus but the Christian community's lack of willingness to share the good news. So the real need is not to pray for souls but for soul-winners.

Robert Coleman expresses the truth very clearly when he states, "No, there is no use to pray vaguely for the world. The world is lost and blind in sin. The only hope for the world is for men to go to them with the Gospel of Salvation, and having won them to the Saviour, not to leave them."[3]

The other side of evangelistic praying is that it not only sends the saved person out but it also enables that person to be a fit channel of God's message. "Prayer has a way of molding us so that God can use us as channels. God's power is Holy," so continue Fish and Conant, "and he cannot compromise his holiness by letting his power flow through an unclean channel."[4]

Prayer time alone leads to paltry paralysis—that is, when prayer becomes an end in itself. What each of us should pray is this: "Father in heaven, forgive me of my laziness and now compel me to be a daily witness for you, bringing men to your Son, my Lord and Savior, Jesus Christ." Then prayer would not become, as it so often is, a substitute for sharing but would be the instrument of getting us obedient to God's Word about witnessing.

A few years ago my wife and I had a new home built. One of the men who worked on the house almost every day was a lost man. Each night I would pray that the Lord would give me the courage to witness to him. The last day he was on the job I decided to do it. He was loading his pickup truck with his materials when I drove up. I approached him and said, "John, may I take a minute and tell you how you can become a Christian?" He said, "Go ahead." Soon we both were leaning over the bed of that truck praying as John gave his heart to Christ.

I saw John a few weeks ago and since his conversion he has given up drinking and has involved his whole family in a church near his home. It so blesses my heart to see the great change in his life.

Scores of people are waiting for someone to talk with them. They will not be saved by prayer only. It will take a little time to speak the word of truth to their hearts. There comes a time to get off our knees and onto our feet. It's worth mentioning again, "Prayer and means must go together. Means without prayer—presumption. Prayer without means—hypocrisy."[5] So says Spurgeon.

7

THE INEFFECTIVE RIGHT
WAY OF DOING NOTHING

Vince Lombardi, the late coach of the Green Bay Packers, said, "Winning is not the most important thing; it's everything." There are those who would disagree with that and I, too, find myself wanting to make several exceptions to that bold declaration. Nevertheless, it is refreshing to find someone who believes that the ultimate goal is being a winner, being successful in attaining the desired end. There are just too many people following the "path of least resistance" philosophy while rationalizing laziness and ineffectiveness.

How terribly true this is in the contemporary church. There is at best a vague understanding of the church's goals and at worst an uncaring attitude about whether the church has any goals or not. Yet the game of church is played again and again without any apparent concern about the church making a viable difference in the world. Things are being done right, according to the many textbooks that are read, but nothing is happening; thus, it is the ineffective right way of doing nothing. Let's look at some areas where this destructive phenomenon is most dangerous.

PROPER PERFORMANCE PRODUCING REGRETTABLE RESULTS

If the devil can just set up false standards for us, he has gone a long way in accomplishing his task. If he can get us to believe that we have done everything just right in our Christian life, irrespective of the results, then he's got us whipped. For if he can get us to sit down and relax on the battlefield of defeat, thinking we have won a victory, we will see no need to fight the enemy any longer. Satan will tell us we held the rifles just right; the strategy was perfect; the artillery was all in place; we cared wonderfully for the wounded; our soldiers were extremely attractive in their new uniforms; the battalions were well organized; and most important of all, the soldiers were all very nice and sincere. We really shouldn't worry that most of our soldiers were either killed or wounded and the enemy continues its triumphant march.

Unquestionably, this has been the devil's successful approach to churches around the world. He has convinced them by insisting that they are successful because they have properly performed the external functions of religion, ignoring the pitiful and regrettable results. God help us to rid ourselves of this cowardly and anemic approach to the joyful task before us.

An educational director of a church I served was talking to me one time about a meeting he had set up to train teachers. It was a miserable flop. Out of more than forty people expected to attend, only six people showed up, and the instructor was a misinformed bore. Said this staff member to me, "What really hurts me is that I did everything just right. The teacher was a state-approved worker; the material was all the recommended literature; and I sent a letter to everyone." Then in a soliloquy of despair he said, "Well, it's hard to believe everything went like this, but at least I did everything right." That's what I call proper performance and regrettable results; the performance becomes a substitute for the results our Lord wants to see. It reminds me of what a friend of mine heard recently from his Russian guide while touring Moscow. The guide said, "We have the greatest agricultural program in the world. We can't understand why it's not working."

Somehow, we are going to have to stop telling ourselves that if we sing a certain kind of music, use a certain kind of literature, and have the right ladies' mission group and men's group, we are an ideal church. We just need to be results conscious and by results I'm talking about people reached and taught by the church. If all our music had to be contrary to what some call high-class music, if our Sunday school had to change its name to something else, if the Women's Missionary Society had to be drastically revolutionized, if we had to start having services several times other than Sunday—if, if, if—if we had to do anything to get the church more conscious of reaching people, which is our Lord's desire for us, we should be willing to do it. If all of this had to be done so that we might stop looking at what we have called proper performance and start alleviating the regrettable results, it would be worth it, would it not?

It's a shame, but some people become enamored with initials and names of organizations and never ask themselves if these are really fulfilling the Great Commission of our Lord. I've even heard churches terribly criticized because they didn't have these organizations even though they were doing more to reach and love people and had obviously greater spiritual results. I'm totally committed to effective organization, but if a church has all of the proper programs and organizations and has pleased the various denominational observers and is not shaking its community for Christ, it is not a successful church. McGavran hits the truth squarely on the head: "Christians are working at winning others to Christ. They look at the community round about them and see men and women who really ought to know Jesus. They bring in reports as to the numbers who have received Christ. They have plans for growth. In other words, they are committed to winning others."[1]

I realize that there are other things besides evangelism, but it is the cutting edge of all that we do. I heard someone say once that "evangelism is to missions what burning is to fire." A church with a Christian mission (should there be any other kind?) has no fire apart from evangelism. In fact, it is the great evangelistic churches that also excel in these other ministries. For when a man really gets burdened about souls, he gets concerned for the total man. Our church once led our denomination in baptisms for twelve consecutive years, and during this time we had a ministry to the deaf, the mentally challenged, and the hungry, as well as a prisoner minister on our staff, all while sending tens of thousands of dollars to the mission field.

One of the finest Christian ladies who ever lived died in an ultramodern and lavishly equipped hospital in Texas. She had undergone a common surgery. She was only forty at her death and the general feeling of those close to the situation was that she died from sheer neglect. One of her dearest friends said in a tearful moment, "Our hospital back home is not new. It's much smaller than this one, too, but I just know Frankie would have made it there because they really care." This is exactly what I'm saying. We must be concerned not only that the church looks good and the programs are all proper and highly recommended but also whether people are loved, won, and discipled in the name of Jesus. Why should anyone stand back and look at a beautiful hospital where very few patients survive and say, "My, what a wonderful hospital"? In fact, no one should say that, because the hospital would be a detriment to society because of the false hope it would give by its very existence—keeping people from where they might get genuine care. So, a church is not brick and mortar, programs and performances, services and sanctuaries. It is where people for whom Jesus died are sought, saved, and sealed by loving Christians in the power of the Holy Spirit. It doesn't matter that what is done is "proper" if the patient does not survive, and it doesn't matter how polished the performance of the church is if the New Testament principles of a church are ignored. The church is to be a hospital for sinners, but too many have become hotels for saints!

No, the ends don't always justify the means. Neither do the means justify failure. If the means are not getting the spiritual ends they should, there must be a willingness to change the means. If performance is genuinely proper, it should bring rewarding not regrettable results. Oh, the ineffective right way of doing nothing.

THE MALAISE OF MEDIOCRITY

In a small town where I once was pastor, there was a man who had a strange reply to people who complained how he might have repaired something at his fix-it shop. His oft-heard response was, "Well, it's better than it was." I wouldn't say his standards were too high, would you?

Far too often this attitude of being satisfied with little or no achievement has prevailed in the contemporary church. Somehow challenge has evaded us. We have become content with business as usual while, with a creative determination, hundreds of new ministries could be found to reach the lost and challenge the converted. And the tragedy is, this mediocrity seems not to disturb millions of church members and even some church leaders.

Years ago, Bernard E. Meland of the University of Chicago wrote concerning this problem:

> The prevailing church model is mediocrity. Its music, its architecture, its prayers, its parish talk, its celebrations are all mediocre. The influence that emanates from its doors, through its ministry, through its preachments, spread mediocrity like a deadening blight over the life of communities. Mediocrity has taken hold of us as a people, when comfort and happiness take priority over all use, the zest of more consequential concerns lanquishes, the dimensions of life shrink to mediocrity. This is the deafening disease of our time.[2]

If that is too harsh, then maybe the words of Dr. E. Y. Mullins, former president of Southern Seminary in Louisville, Kentucky, will communicate to us more appropriately: "The chief difficulty is that God's people have been content to think in terms of conventional Christianity, comfortable and smug, without a sense of conquest or ambition for great things. Jesus did not set out to catch sparrows or subdue rabbits."[3]

Chesterton said, "Jesus was a lion tamer." The application is obvious.

Here again, the church finds itself guilty of doing things the so-called right way no matter how ineffective it is, then complimenting itself when it really needs to bow in humble repentance.

I see this time and again in meetings we feel obligated to have. Almost no one comes and low attendance is blamed on some unavoidable circumstance. Many preachers have shared with me similar experiences. We travel hundreds of miles to speak at a meeting involving several churches only to discover that no serious effort was made to get people to attend. And those in charge don't seem to be overly concerned even though much good could have been accomplished if people had been there. It almost appears that some meetings are held for the meeting's sake rather than for the people's sake.

Surely God's people ought to do everything they can to make every meeting a glorious success. If the meeting has a purpose, it should be done right and everyone qualified to attend should be compelled to be there. Too often after these wasted sessions, someone will say, "Well, only a handful came, but if just one person was helped it was worth it."

That's true, but when hundreds were *not* helped because of poor organization and sheer laziness, that statement seems cheap.

Let's not approve our mediocrity. Let's become results conscious. Let's never forget that programs without people are of no value at all. Let's determine to do everything as if we are doing it for Jesus. That will demand our best efforts mentally, spiritually, and physically.

Every church in America fits under one of the following three categories: (1) Some, but sadly a small number, are risk takers. They are launching into their communities doing whatever it takes to win people to Jesus; (2) More, unfortunately, are caretakers, content with mediocrity, trying to maintain what they have; (3) The ultimate result is that many churches are now undertakers, doing little more than burying their dead.

To really reach our nation for Christ, we must realize that doing things right means winning people to Christ. Let's not worship the ineffective programs while a world goes unreached and untaught. It's foolish to be polishing the brass rails while the ship is sinking. To paraphrase the words of Jesus, "What will it profit a church if it should gain proper programs and its community loses its soul?"

8

CULTURAL HEAT WITHOUT SPIRITUAL LIGHT

Surely this has to be one of the most subtle of all the substitutes because it is such a part of the life style of millions of people. There is difficulty in distinguishing between what is done for cultural reasons and what is done for genuine Christian reasons. The subtlety is so powerful because the thing being done is apparently good and has all the flavor of religious activity. Of course, as was amplified in an earlier chapter, religion has far too often been a substitute for true Christian dedication. Therefore, religious duties often take the place of real evangelism.

Much of what goes on in our country could be explained more by cultural and social interest than by heaven-felt Christian discipleship. Sometimes the motivation for activity is the sheer desire for entertainment. There is certainly nothing wrong with wholesome Christian entertainment, but it must not be confused with real Christian involvement.

Scores of Christians will attend a function, but they themselves never function as soldiers of the Cross. These millions of people eagerly and gratefully discover these activities and use them as substitutes for being involved in evangelism. Once again, evangelism, the primary thing we are to do, gets put aside with no more than secondary consideration. Many churches should put on their marquee "Fun, Food, Fellowship," the unholy trinity of selfish satisfaction.

Let's look at some of these cultural aspects that often give people a sense of Christian involvement but may not be Christian at all. They may be good things to do, but their danger is that often they become the total Christian expression of those involved. Here they are.

ALL-DAY *SANGINS*

One of the phenomena of Christian activity is the love that so many in traditional churches have for meetings where there is nothing but singing. I call them *sangins* because I have heard the meetings described that way so many times. I once thought they were isolated to the southern states and the Bible Belt, but as I've traveled extensively in the last several years, I've discovered that they're everywhere. Those in the South, however, do seem to have a distinctive nature.

I remember in a small church where I served as pastor at the beginning of my ministry it was a struggle to get many to attend. But when the monthly *sangin* came along, people poured out of the hills and valleys, the byways, and highways to attend that music fest. And you should have heard the old songs of the faith that were sung, "Jimmy Ain't Crippled No More," "Grandma Is Still Crocheting Socks for

Tony," "Mother's Pickin' Lilies in Heaven." No, not really but almost.

Now I may have taken a little privilege of exaggeration for the sake of communication, but some of the songs were really so disrespectful that I decided to not even mention their titles in this book. One of the more disturbing aspects of the meeting was that many of the quartets who came to sing seemed less than sincere. This was especially true of the many who I knew never once went to church. They merely traveled across the country as so-called gospel entertainers. Also, some of them had personal lives that were consistently improper; yet the crowds came and packed the little churches where they performed. I suppose it really didn't bother the crowd that many of the singing groups didn't go to church and lived less than discreet lives because they had the same kinds of habits. The *sangin* phenomenon almost became a church within itself.

After many of these occasions, I observed those who attended coming out of the sessions with tears running down their faces. Many of them were members of churches around the area, but they never, or rarely, attended. They would stand outside after the rousing music and tell one racial joke after another. They would say, "One of them better never try to come into my church." The circle of folks around would say, "Yeah, that's true with me too!"

As a young, unsuspecting preacher, I couldn't balance it all. They loved the songs about Jesus, but they didn't have the Spirit of Christ. They would gather in great numbers to sing but would not show up to go visiting and witnessing. They would cry over those in heaven, but made no effort to help folks get there. *What's wrong?* I asked myself.

Well, the simple but disturbing answer soon came. These people (obviously there were exceptions) didn't love Jesus. They loved that kind of music because of their cultural conditioning. Their commitment was to a form, not to the absolute lordship of Jesus Christ. They would scorn the idea of making an effort to share their faith but would—without question—be at the next "all-day *sangin.*" The tragedy is they thought that made them super-Christians.

Now, let me say some things for the sake of clarification and fairness. I love gospel music and especially the old songs. I even love the ones with honest emotion in the message and melody. Too much of our music is dry. That's my cultural preference, not an indication of my Christian commitment. But we never lie more than when we sing!

The more sophisticated often have the same tendency. You see, the danger is not in the kind of culture, but in the loyalty to that culture apart from a higher loyalty to Christ. It's possible for someone to be more in love with high-church music than with Jesus. Numbers of Christians are attracted to a particular church because its form matches their cultural conditioning. And that's all right. Not everyone worships in the same way, but it's possible to be excited about rural music or the music of Bach and not be an active witness for Jesus. Too many are committed to a style instead of a person. Their cultural backs are scratched and they feel they enjoyed it because of their Christian dedication, while it was merely their interest in music.

I am appreciative of our music director in the church I serve. He does everything from a Bach anthem to a Gaither gospel. I've seen him present music I knew he personally disliked, but he thought it might reach some people, so he did it. That's really Christian commitment when a person becomes bigger than his culture. Someone once questioned some less than high-church music he selected, and he responded, "Well, you know I didn't care for it either, but it's not important whether I like it or you like it. The thing that is important is that we reach people for Jesus with our music." Then he added, "We don't really sing music for music; we sing it for Christian ministry." Amen! How true!

All up and down the cultural gamut, there is that problem—cultural heat instead of spiritual warmth. The same is true with much of the contemporary music today. Many of these groups who hold massive concerts love Jesus and preach the gospel. But too many sing more for the praise of people than for the applause of heaven. There must come to each of us the realization that we are to be disciples of Jesus Christ first—above all things, including our culture, our preferences, our prejudices, our likes or dislikes. Time and again Christians feel they have shown dedication while truly they have only satisfied their cultural curiosity.

What a substitute all of this becomes for reaching people across every cultural strata. Let's never forget this. There is only one kind of person in the world and that's a person for whom Jesus died. He said that *all* of us should go for *all* of them in his name.

DECORATION DAY

I'll not spend much time with this because, even though the practice of Decoration Day occurs in almost all fifty states, it might be new to some readers. I use it here because it illustrates so well what I'm saying at this point.

What is Decoration Day? It is an annual practice of many Christians choosing one Sunday when they all meet at a church near a cemetery and place flowers on the graves of departed loved ones. That is, they decorate the burial places with flowers. Associated with this is an afternoon of singing and eating.

I remember serving in an area where this was most prominent. My church was not the nearby church. So on that day, dozens of my members and members of other churches would miss their own services to attend Decoration Day at the church near or even adjacent to the cemetery. The pastor of that church told me that almost half of the people who came to Decoration Day were not active church members anywhere and never intended to be, although they claimed to be Christians. They felt that this was an act of great Christian dedication.

Not only is that fact alarming but also, the people who did attend from other churches did that more faithfully than anything else they did in their own churches; they were especially negligent in the area of witnessing.

Why am I reporting all of this? Because millions of people comfort themselves with the idea that because they are busy associating themselves with the business around the church, they are doing something for Christ. Certainly, every Christian should be busy at the church, but when one attends functions for cultural reasons while using the excuse of time for not showing up for visitation, there is an obvious hypocrisy and inconsistency.

Decoration Day is just one of many illustrations of this danger. I'm certain that in liturgical churches or in churches with less formal services, there is that problem—cultural heat without spiritual light. A lost person may be attracted by cultural activity, but a Christian should be excited about what honors Christ and brings persons to his cross.

CONDEMNATION WITHOUT COMPASSION

Disraeli said, "It is easier to be critical than correct." How true! Of course one could be both, but so often the harsh critic is wrong, if not always in substance certainly in attitude.

Culture will often make a person extremely critical of certain things. It is at this point that some of the finest Christians on earth trip and fall. They feel that to condemn sin is the ultimate goal in the Christian experience. Often the sins they most harshly criticize are not the sins Jesus most criticized.

When Jesus was asked to reduce the law to its greatest substance, he said to "love the Lord thy God with all thy heart. . . . And . . . love thy neighbour as thyself" (Mark 12:30–31). Jesus himself was always compassionate before he was critical. Therefore, the greatest responsibility of a Christian is to love. And the finest way to love a lost person is to lead that person to know Jesus Christ as his or her personal Lord and Savior.

Too often culture leads us to make some sins cardinal sins. Usually the sins of the flesh are picked. Let me quickly say that there needs to be more, many more, preachers and other Christians who stand against the impure sins of our day and for the sterling life the Bible proclaims. The issue I'm making here is that there is a tendency to speak with condemnation before compassion and often without compassion at all. Jesus taught against the sins of the flesh, but more often he taught about the dangers of the sins of the spirit.

The religious hypocrites of Jesus' day called him in contempt a "friend of sinners." Have you ever taken a serious look at Luke 15? Most people have missed the emphasis completely. Jesus spoke that entire chapter out of response to a critical spirit on the part of the Pharisees and scribes who said, "This man receiveth sinners, and eateth with them" (v. 2).

Jesus, we know, responded to the criticism by telling three parables: the lost sheep, the lost coin, and the lost son. Every story ends successfully. The lost sheep is rescued, the coin is found, and the lost son returns home. Jesus concluded with the whole purpose of the parables when he told of the attitude of the older son who begrudged the good treatment of the wayward son. You see, the whole chapter is really pointing to the story of the older son, whom Jesus was comparing to the Pharisees. It is interesting to note that only the incident of the older son ends unsuccessfully. Verse 28 says that "he was angry [like the Pharisees, because Jesus loves the sinners like the father loves the prodigal son], and would not go in." We are never told that he came back to the father.

How interesting! There is hope for a person lost through stupidity like a wandering sheep or through carelessness like a lost coin or through rebellion like the prodigal son; for the critical person who refuses to love the lost, there is no hope. He stays outside.

Yes, there is hope even for that person, but the lesson of Jesus is strong. A critical, condemning person like the older son is often more hopeless than the vilest sinner for he is blind to his own damning attitude. Jesus says in that chapter that a person who condemns the sinner without loving the person may be the worst sinner of all and greatest in danger of the judgment of God.

The Pharisees, religious nuts blinded by their cultural loyalties, are like too many in our day. They find it easier to criticize the sinner and those who love the sinner than to do anything right themselves. Criticism is too often a substitute for performance.

I once sat in a ministerial alliance being critical, as were most of the other preachers, of a certain activity the young people of our city were engaged in. One of the men moved that we pass a resolution against the activity. I voted, as did most of the other men, for the resolution. It was voted to send the resolution to the high-school principal.

Finally, a perceptive elderly preacher representing one of the most conservative denominations stood up to speak. He said, "Gentlemen, I'm probably the most conservative preacher in this room, but right now I feel like a Pharisee. The resolution is right. I voted for it, but let's not send it yet. Let's first start a program to reach our young people for the Lord. Let's all get together and have a citywide youth revival or something to show our love before we express this criticism." He then looked at each of us with the penetrating eyes of a prophet and said, "Men, have you shared Jesus very many times with the ringleaders of this group?" No one could say that they had shared Jesus with any of them. We felt ashamed. His point was made.

Light on sin? Never! Yet, first of all, love the sinner with an arm of compassion, knowing that sin is best conquered not by the vote of a ministerial alliance but by the indwelling presence of Jesus in a heart and life. If enough of Jesus gets in, the sin will get out. Plus, it's not possible to get someone to cease some sin that disturbs us through our harsh complaints, while leaving them outside the life of Christ. When you fish for people you bait your hook with love.

I heard about a pastor who took a layman in a major city to share Jesus. His approach was rather unique—the two went from storefront to storefront with a squeegee and a spray bottle, offering to wash the windows. They came upon a bar and entered. Seeing the bartender, the pastor said, "We would like to wash your windows if we may." Perplexed, the bartender replied, "Sure, but why?" "We are showing Jesus' love in a practical way," was the pastor's reply.

A lady sitting at the bar turned to the pastor. "What did you say?" she asked. "We are showing Jesus' love in a practical way." Then, with a look of loneliness and heartache, she asked him, "Would your church welcome someone like me?" In six months, this unchurched lady was saved and active in that church. Compassion counts.

Apparently, many feel the more condemning they are the less they must be about the Father's business. There is a place for condemnation, but there is a bigger place for compassion. Anger is never a substitute for sharing the good news of Jesus Christ.

Cultural idiosyncrasies may not be the same as Christian commitment. Pray, as I want to pray, "Father, help me to hate the sins and love the sinners. Help me to share Jesus with them, for if they take your Son as their Savior, sin will be an ugly thing to them. Forgive me when I've talked so much about others—I've not talked to others about you."

Subtle substitutes find their way into the lives of the best of us. Let's get back to proclaiming the good news. Above and before all else, that's real evangelism.

9

THE TIRED PASTOR AND
THE WEARY LORD

To be called "Pastor" is music to my ears. I became a pastor of a Southern Baptist church when I was a teenager and continued for twenty-eight years. "Happiness is being a Pastor" quipped a little sign on my desk. I can identify with what Spurgeon said to his son, "If God ever calls you to preach, don't condescend to be the prime minister of England." Amen and amen! Even though I am now in vocational evangelism, I still feel and think like a pastor. I still make hospital calls, counsel, and officiate at weddings and funerals. As a pastor I was often called by others a "pastor-evangelist." Now perhaps I am an "evangelist-pastor."

I love my fellow pastors and enjoy their company. They are, as a group, the most honest, courageous, selfless men of integrity on earth. The vast majority of them feel a real purpose and mission in their calling of God. They would be willing to fight unto the death to benefit the work of the Master.

As those of any other profession, they have their misgivings and frustrations. Much of the frustration they sense is the immensity of their responsibility, wondering how to get it all done and still be the men of God they so much want to be. They know that above all things they are to be good preachers and shepherds of their flocks. They hunger for more time to do just the basics of a ministering servant of Christ.

Charles McKay is right when he says in *The Call of the Harvest,* "Preachers are called to preach! Jesus came preaching. God commanded Jonah, 'Go . . . preach the preaching that I bid thee.' The power of the preaching of the preacher lies in the depth of his spiritual life. People will not excuse the man in the pulpit if he fails to preach."[1] Then McKay quotes 1 Corinthians 1:21: "It pleased God by the foolishness of preaching to save them."[2]

Even though pastors would agree with this, they find themselves so burdened with businesslike duties that they scarcely have time to minister. Satan so often tries to get the pastor involved in everything besides that for which he has been called. He substitutes trips, committees, and sometimes even honors that need attention for the best work of God's man. I hope this chapter will be an encouragement to pastors as they seek to put first things first.

MEETINGS THAT MATTER

Because of the cooperative spirit of pastors, they often find themselves unable to say no. They attend meeting after meeting after meeting. It reminds me of a lady who was very willing to be involved in clubs and various organizations. She was constantly busy attending one or more of these meetings. It is said that when she died her epitaph read, "Here lies Mary Jones. She was *clubbed* to death."

Too many pastors have been "clubbed" to death. That is, they have found themselves going to every meeting available out of a sense of helpfulness and loyalty and returning home so tired, they haven't adequate strength to be about the main task before them. One pastor jokingly said that he no longer wanted to go to heaven because he was afraid he would have "to serve on the appropriations committee there."

One time I served as chairman of an associational committee and was a member of another. I was chairman of a state committee of my denomination, while serving on another state committee. I was on the executive board for the state convention and the meeting place was a five-hour drive (before the 55 mph speed limit) from the church I served. I was a member of the Chamber of Commerce and the Rotary Club and chairman of the Blood-Donor Drive— all at the same time. It was enough to make a man feel led to start a work in Acapulco.

In the midst of all this I realized how tired I was and how weary the Lord must be of it. They were all good things, but not the best things. I've even driven ten hours to speak forty minutes. I used these things to be a witness, but I discovered it was not the most effective approach to successful spiritual leadership. People appreciate seeing the pastor involved in certain civic concerns, but they really want a man who is in touch with God. We must be mastered by the Master, not the meetings. I remembered the words of Carl Bates, one of the Southern Baptists' great preachers, "God did not call us to be second-rate public relations men, but first-class preachers."

I immediately altered my schedule to try to give my best self for the most essential work—reaching people for Christ.

When Dwight L. Moody was being considered by a ministers group for a third crusade in a particular city, someone objected, "Why get Moody again? Does he have a monopoly on God?" Said another pastor in reply, "No, but God has a monopoly on Moody." God's men ought to indeed be men of God. That's not easy when meetings weigh us down.

Even meetings at one's own church can master a schedule. I have made the mistake of thinking I had to attend every committee meeting, but fortunately I got over that. Attend the essential ones, like deacons meetings, but, Pastor, let your gifted laymen carry on most of the others and give yourself time to be about what you do best. The late Adrian Rogers, pastor of the great Bellevue Baptist Church in Memphis, Tennessee, said something to a gathering of preachers that was a help to me. Said he, "A preacher who is available all of the time is not worth anything when he is." Even though one could carry that to an extreme, it is a good thought to ponder. A preacher is like an automobile; he needs to stop for refueling before he can go farther. We all know that for the preacher refueling is found in the Word of God and on bended knee before the throne. As one wise pastor said, "If you dip water out of the same pail, it will run dry." We need time for spiritual refilling.

SEEKING STATUS INSTEAD OF SOULS

Here Satan is especially effective because he knows that all of us pastors want to be what we're expected to be. But the temptation to seek status is a subtle substitute indeed. Sometimes we assume that since we have come to a church of some size we need to act distant and untouchable. We begin to feel that our people expect us to be on a pedestal of reverential display, so we sit there expecting the admiration and accolades of those around us, like mannequins in the denominational showcase displaying our clerical attire. Sometimes it even changes our voice to a lower octave and our words have a taint of polish and formality of coldness. When this sort of thing happens to us, we then discover that we have become men of position and not mission. And a preacher without a mission becomes a tragic picture of frail and defeated humanity. What then is a preacher?

Surely there is no better description of what the church's preacher truly is than the one Paul the Apostle outlines in 2 Corinthians chapter 4. Paul began by saying, "Therefore, seeing we have this ministry. . . ." Who is the "we" mentioned twelve times in this chapter? He was referring to his fellow preachers of the gospel—to us. The word *ministry* indicates that Paul felt we preachers were called of God to be about something and, while this passage primarily relates to Paul and his preacher friends, it reveals characteristics of the true preacher of any age.

1. A limited man with unlimited power. Listen to the words: "But we have this treasure in earthen vessels, that the excellency of the power may be of God, and not of us" (v. 7). What a strange combination—earthen vessels and God's power. But that's what we are. We preachers are earthen vessels, clay jars, mud pots, without inexhaustible strength or claims to personal value. Paul refused to use any other metaphor that might compare us to pitchers of brass or vases of silver or goblets of gold— we preachers are just products of the earth.

We are not celestial ecclesiastics with wings of angelic span or the incarnation of clerical divinity. Our calling, as special and singularly significant as it is, does not insulate us from the limitations of the flesh or the imperfections of being the sons of Adam. And yet in us, God has chosen to invest a divine call and empower us with his Holy Spirit. Why? That the attention might be on the contents and not on the vessel, that the "excellency of the power may be of God, and not of us." Sometimes I think that we preachers are especially earthly.

My grandfather Lucky, for instance, was an earthen vessel as a preacher with emphasis on the earthen—seventh-grade education, no theological training, improper English. He didn't split infinitives; he mutilated them. But he had his eyes on the treasure. When he preached, heaven opened and it seemed the angels would sing the invitation and sinners would be converted and evil men and women would fall weeping before a holy God. He was a man who majored on the treasure and not on the vessel. People who are in the poverty of sin need a man with the treasure of divine calling to make them rich in grace. He was, as we are, a limited man with unlimited power.

An earthly friend of mine, newly called to minister but with a genuine commitment to our Lord, preached in Washington State one night on Nicodemus, but pronounced the name Nigh-cod-a-mus; he mispronounced the name all the way through and twenty-one people were saved. (He had power because he realized he was God's man.) Our diction is not as vital as our dedication. Our disposition is as important as our dispensation.

Now we ought to keep the vessel clean, educate it, culture it, but if we aren't careful we could become glossy, well-shaped, empty, and powerless vessels. The major emphasis needs to be on the treasure, on the calling, on the work of God in our lives, on his presence and filling, on his enduement and empowering, not on us, the earthen, ever-crumbling vessel. At best, the earthen vessel is a dirt container, but at the least—the treasure is still a treasure of inestimable value.

Fellow pastors, if we lose our polish from the vessel, we must forever retain the power of the treasure. The limitations of the vessel will never limit us as long as the power of the treasure empowers us.

Look again to what the preacher is.

2. *A submissive man with a supreme message.* "For we preach not ourselves, but Christ Jesus the Lord; and ourselves your servants for Jesus' sake" (2 Cor. 4:5).

We are servants of God for the people. We are not career men seeking selfish goals for personal gain; neither are we men expressing our views behind the protection of the pulpit. The issue is not our views; it is God's good news the folks in the pew are concerned about. You see, if the ministry is the avenue we've chosen to crusade our doubts, disbeliefs, opinions, and theological wanderings, or even our learning, we need to go out into a desert place for a while and let a coal from the altar burn in our soul until self is burned out and the truth of Christ becomes forged steel in our bones. Not ourselves, but Christ.

When you were first saved, wasn't your main thought, *Why me, Lord? Why would you save a wretch like me?* Then God called you to preach. Again, you said, "Why me, Lord?" But, as time passed, and another guy got that chance you had your eye on, and you were overlooked for such and such assignment, you said, "Why not me, Lord?"

You were called by God to serve him. When a man preaches that the Bible is partly the Word of God, he's preaching himself. When a man preaches that there is some way other than the bloodstained banner of the cross, he's preaching himself. When a man says Christ is the best way to heaven, he's preaching himself because the Bible says there is "none other name under heaven given among men, whereby we must be saved" (Acts 4:12). He's the Only Way. When a man preaches that it's acceptable to involve yourself in any habit (as long as you're responsible), he's preaching himself because the Bible says the body is the temple of the Holy Spirit. When a man says Jesus is not really coming again, he must be preaching himself because the Book tells us he "cometh with ten thousands of his saints" (Jude 14). No wonder Dr. A. T. Robertson comments on this verse referring to preaching self, "Surely as poor and disgusting a topic as a preacher can find."

"When God commands to take the trumpet," wrote John Milton in a famous passage, "and blow a dolorous or jarring blast, it lies not in man's will what he shall say, or what he shall conceal."

If we cannot preach the Book, we shouldn't use the pulpit to display our dead souls because we as God's preachers do not preach ourselves but Christ Jesus the Lord. We have submitted to him and are under his orders, and if we can't cope with that, we are probably volunteers instead of draftees and should be discharged from the army of God. Brethren, don't throw the rotten apples of your own undisciplined commitment at your congregation, but gather fresh fruit from the tree of life and feed them.

A young lady once went to Will Rogers for counseling and said, "Mr. Rogers, what can I do about pride? Every time I look in the mirror, I think I'm beautiful." Will Rogers replied, "Honey, that's not pride; that's a mistake."

Men, if we think the ministry and message are ours,

we're just mistaken. God's message is our only message, and we are his ambassadors.

Martin Luther's preaching aroused the church from a thousand years' slumber during the Dark Ages—the devil's millennium. It is easy to understand why when we discover how Luther preached. He said, "I preach as though Christ were crucified yesterday; rose again from the dead today; and is coming back to earth tomorrow." It was all Christ. Not ourselves—Christ! Paul was not ashamed of the gospel of Christ for it is the power of God, and if you and I don't submit ourselves to the total truth of that gospel, we have no power. Submissive men with a supreme message: Christ Jesus is Lord. One pastor prayed after awakening to what his preaching had been, "O God, forgive me for parading my learning when I should have been leading men to thee." Billy Sunday once said, "In one of my first sermons I had sentences as long as your arm. If a Greek professor tried to pronounce some of the words, his jaw would squeak for a week. I preached that sermon and it felt like a dud. I didn't kill. I knew something was wrong, so I took out the old Gospel gun and loaded her up with rock salt, ipecac, barded wire, carpet tacks, and rough on rats. I lowered the hindsight and blazed away and the gangs been ducking and the devils been hunting his hole ever since." God gives us more preachers who are willing to speak plainly and boldly. Cautious preaching never convicts.

Also, God's preacher is a man of:

3. *Troubled living but a triumphant life.* Paul said, "We are troubled on every side, yet not distressed; we are perplexed, but not in despair; persecuted, but not forsaken; cast down, but not destroyed" (2 Cor. 4:8–9).

The sincere preacher, because he speaks the strong,

unbending truths of God, may find the going rough. Paul and Silas and other friends found it so. The people of the Old Testament pleaded with their prophets, "Speak unto us smooth things" (Isa. 30:10). It has been said that the disease of modern preaching is its search for popularity.

Of course, some will fall away from strong convictions. But men, if we avoid the trouble we will miss the triumph. A man who stands with Christ may know trouble, but his life shall be one of triumph. People may be difficult and critical, but the way of obedience is the way of victory—"Cast down, but not destroyed." The destroying comes when we refuse to be cast down. There is no price too costly to be the pure men of God he has commissioned us to be.

Recently, I learned of a young preacher who preached the truth but was having trouble with one especially critical parishioner. This fellow's favorite expression was, "Great day!" In a business meeting or wherever, he would express himself with, "Great day!"

One Sunday morning the young preacher said as he arrived at the pulpit, "I'm preaching on the text 'And Jesus fed five men with five thousand loaves of bread and two thousand fishes.'"

The critical brother jumped up and said, "Great day, that's no miracle, I could do that!"

The young preacher was shattered and couldn't even preach his sermon. The next Sunday, out of spite, he announced correctly, "And Jesus fed five thousand men with five loaves and two fishes." He looked right at the outspoken member and said, "And I guess you could do that too?"

"I certainly could," he said.

"How?" the preacher questioned.

"With what was left over from last Sunday," the man insisted.

Well, we have our troubles, but we have the victory through Jesus Christ our Lord. "Persecuted, but not forsaken." The glorious triumphs are worth the troubles.

Furthermore, the preacher is a man with:

4. *An earthly commitment and a heavenly vision.* Paul said we are doing "all things . . . for your sakes . . . for which cause we faint not" (2 Cor. 4:15–16). We have an earthly job to do from which we cannot shrink. We are not sophisticated prima donnas on pedestals of false dignity. We are workers, servants dedicated to making whatever sacrifice is necessary to get the job done because the work of the preacher has eternal consequences as Paul said in 2 Corinthians 4:17, "Our light affliction, which is but for a moment, worketh for us a far more exceeding and eternal weight of glory." It reminds me of Paul's words in Romans: "For I reckon that the sufferings of this present time are not worthy to be compared with the glory which shall be revealed in us" (8:18).

The countryfolk sang in years gone by, "This world is not my home. I'm just a passing through. . . . I can't feel at home in this world anymore." That may be other-worldly, but there is another world, you know! Jesus said, "If it were not so, I would have told you" (John 14:2). We should be totally committed to the life of Christ lived out on this earth but always realize there is more to come!

Recently, I studied afresh the stoning of Stephen in the book of Acts. Stephen, a faithful prophet, looked up and saw Christ "standing." All the other references say Christ is seated at the right hand of God. This is the only reference we have to tell us how Christ receives a preacher of his. Stephen, weary from his preaching and dying from the stoning, looked up—as you will do, faithful servant—and saw Christ standing, ready to greet him and love him and say, "Well done." Catch that vision. You'll catch fire! Men, preach the truth as Stephen did whatever the cost, but keep looking up because one day when you lay down the sword, you'll come face-to-face with a standing Christ with outstretched arms ready to receive his faithful preacher.

The great hymnwriter Isaac Watts put it cleverly in his hymn "Am I a Soldier of the Cross?":

> *Am I a soldier of the Cross?*
> *A foll'wer of the Lamb?*
> *And shall I fear to own His cause*
> *Or blush to speak His name?*
> *Must I be carried to the skies*
> *On flow'ry beds of ease,*
> *While others fought to earn the prize,*
> *And sailed through bloody seas?*
> *Sure I must fight if I would reign—*
> *Increase my courage, Lord!*
> *I'll bear the toil, endure the pain,*
> *Supported by Thy Word.*

Well, that's what a preacher is, but why are some preachers of the gospel not as enthusiastic as they ought to be about their work? What unique dangers do all of us face as preachers, pastors, evangelists, or denominational servants?

FAMILIARITY BREEDS CONTEMPT

Sometimes our closeness to the institutional things of Jesus can cause us to lose our excitement for the real person of Jesus. I've been way out in the country with some rural people and have been more enriched by their relationship to Christ than by someone who is vocationally involved in Christian work. Why? Because the pastor or other vocational worker becomes so involved in the planning part that we can miss the pleasing part. We get so busy working for Jesus that we don't stop long enough to let Jesus work in us. The responsibilities of the position are so demanding that we miss the joy of the mission. The vessel is so tired that we can't clearly appreciate the treasure.

Jess Moody in his book *A Drink at Joel's Place* makes a profound observation in this regard. Dr. Moody relates how he has become a successful pastor of a large and growing church. He mentions his honors and prestigious positions on various boards and agencies. He tells us that he has even received honorary degrees from universities. He says that it is so different from his earlier life as an excited young preacher of a small church in Texas. Then he says something every preacher on earth must consider: "I miss the sound of sandled feet."

Men, whatever else we miss in our ministry we must not miss "the sound of sandled feet." Jesus—sweet, precious, and real—must be our life, our all, whether our church is big or small or whether our name is known or unknown. We can never allow Satan to get us to looking proud at our position while being blind to our mission. The word *sincere* is from the Latin *sincérus,* which means "without wax," genuine, sincere, authentic, real. How I pray that every preacher will not only be doctrinally sound, but also sincere—sincerely in love with Jesus.

A bell ringer for a large cathedral in France had the responsibility of sounding a melody twice a day from the tower of the great church building. He would so ably ring the various carillons that people would stop by the hundreds across several miles to hear the beautiful songs of inspiration as they wafted across the winds of the great city. Many people testified that these melodies gave them strength to meet the demands of the day. The ringer of the bells had performed this ministry for twenty years. The sound was so loud where he rang the bells, it eventually caused him to become deaf. For the last four years he had brought joy to the hearts of others, but he himself never heard a note.

O my fellow pastors, beware lest you get so close to the bells you miss the music. Because it is in the hearing of the music that you are strengthened to fight for the faith and win the crown. Someone said of Dr. Charles Taylor, once president of Wake Forest College, that "the Good News which he preaches to others was first of all the best of all news to his own soul."[3]

Of course the matter of position is not only an issue in regard to pastors and denominational workers, but also to positions within the church. I would like to insert a word of caution for laymen. Sometimes when a person becomes chairman of a committee, or the treasurer, or an usher, or a deacon, he begins to get a little heady. He becomes impressed with position more than his mission. He is willing to serve in order that he might rule. He will show up at the deacons meeting to vote on how to spend a hundred dollars but won't show up on visitation night to lead a soul to Christ. He is impressed with his position but not propelled by his mission.

Philip was one of the very first deacons in the New Testament. He was set apart by men to do certain tasks to allow the apostles to spend more time in study and prayer. It is interesting to note that we are never told that Philip did one thing his position as deacon demanded, but he did extremely well what his mission demanded. For instance, he stopped the eunuch from Ethiopia and led him to give his heart and life to Christ and baptized him. Then, the Bible says, "He preached in all the cities, till he came to Caesarea" (Acts 8:40).

You see, people had one thing in mind for Philip, but before they had their ordaining hands upon Philip's head, God had touched his heart. Long before Philip had a position he had a mission, and he was determined to be a witness for Christ. How refreshing it is to see a person more concerned with his Christian mission—evangelism—than with his position.

Deacons have been and are now some of my dearest friends on earth. I have worked with hundreds of them. They get chided as we preachers do through humorous stories and epigrams.

One time in an evangelistic crusade the evangelist stopped the invitation and asked for every Christian to witness to the person next to him or her. A small boy turned to the gentleman standing near him and said, "Sir, do you know Jesus as your personal Savior?" Very condescendingly the man looked down at the little boy and replied, "Why, son, I'm an ordained deacon." With all the innocence in the world, the little boy responded, "Mister, it don't matter what you've done. God will save you anyway."

Well, even we preachers have to be grateful for that fact.

Here's the truth in a nutshell. Deacons, pastors, church leaders, or vocational Christian workers must never allow their position to rob them of the joy of serving people and winning the richest or the poorest to Christ. Long before people gave us (I realize God was in it too) a position, Christ had called us to a mission—to reach the lost for Christ.

Take caution, for the subtlety of Satan is a fearful thing. He will get us impressed with ourselves while encouraging us to be too busy to get about the task of bringing our world to the foot of the cross.

HOW IS THE FIRE REKINDLED?

What if the position has overwhelmed us? What if we find ourselves burdened with so much church work we don't have time to do the work of the church? What can be done to regain that vital union and hear again "the sound of sandled feet"? What, indeed, rekindles the fire in our life and ministry?

Let me answer by telling this. The Home Mission Board (now the North American Mission Board) of the Southern Baptist Convention asked me to serve in a workshop on revival. We met in a large conference room at Southwestern Baptist Theological Seminary in Fort Worth, Texas. Several pastors, denominational leaders, and seminary professors were there. The last night of the workshop we were to have a banquet on the campus.

Robert Naylor, the soon-to-retire president of the seminary, was asked to speak to us. He began like this: "Many times a preacher boy here will say to me, 'Dr. Naylor, what do you do when in your heart it grows cold?'" He said, "I always answer by telling him that on occasion when I was pastor of Travis Avenue Baptist Church I would find myself cold. It seemed to come so often on a Saturday just the day before I needed to be ready to preach. So, I would get in my car and go out to a house where I knew a lost man lived. I would share Christ with him and watch him be born spiritually as he gave his heart to Christ."

Then, Dr. Naylor concluded, "I would get back in my car and would sing all the way home. The cold had been melted by the fire of the joy God gives a preacher when he sees people saved. Nothing warms up a preacher or his preaching like leading a man to Jesus."

That's it! That's it exactly! When it seems that the inner life is cold and the day of enthusiasm gone, go out and share Jesus with a dear lost one and the fire of God will blaze anew in your heart and in mine. The other things we have to do may be called important by those around us, but there is nothing on earth more important to do than to win a person to Christ Jesus.

McGavran firmly states, "The minister's first task is to grow skillful in personal evangelism, then take his people, one by one, and let them learn by doing."[4] I believe he is right.

When we as pastors get so tired we don't do that, the Lord becomes weary. Let's not be a tired pastor with a weary Lord, but let's be a new burning evangel with a glad Father. There is no substitute for that. "Some soul for thee, some soul for thee, this is my earnest plea."

Andrew Murray said, "God has no more precious gift to a church or an age than a man who lives as the embodiment of His will and inspires those around him with the faith of what grace can do."[5] The preacher ought to be that person.

Dr. B. H. Carroll, once preaching to preachers on the text "Magnify Mine Office," closed his message with these words that could be your theme and mine as modern preachers of the gospel·

> I magnify my office, O my God, as I get nearer home. I can say more truthfully every year, I thank God that he put me in this office; I thank him that he would not let me have any other; that he shut me up to this glorious work. And when I get home among the blessed on the bank of everlasting deliverance, and look back toward time and all of its clouds, and sorrow, and pains and privations, I expect to stand up and shout for joy, that down there in the fog and mists, down there in the dust and in the struggle, God let me be a preacher. I magnify my office in life; I magnify it in death; I magnify it in heaven; I magnify it, whether poor or rich, whether sick or well, whether strong or weak, anywhere, everywhere among all people. Lord God, I am glad that I am a preacher, that I am a preacher of the glorious gospel of Jesus Christ.

What is a preacher? A limited person with unlimited power, a submissive person with a supreme message, one of troubled living but a triumphant life, a person with an earthly commitment and a heavenly vision. I'm glad to be one.

Let's above all things be pure servaants of God who give ourselves daily to Christ's authority. May it always be said of us that because we lived, others were brought to the Master. Evangelism is the Lord's heartbeat. If we major here, he will never be weary of us.

10

COUNTING HEADS INSTEAD OF CHANGING LIVES

O bviously, Jesus was concerned that every person possible be reached with the message of salvation. He, himself, while on the earth, spent laborious hours walking to the various population centers to preach the gospel. He loved people and immensely enjoyed their fellowship. He only separated himself from the gathering crowds when he physically had to—for the special times he needed to be alone with the Father. He not only got involved to reach people but he also time and again sent his disciples out telling them to go house to house. Then he left with us the command to go into all the world. Jesus was concerned with numbers—that is, a number of persons.

There are those who strongly criticize others who have genuine concern for reaching the masses. The criticism is that they ought to be truly concerned for just one or a few, not for a numerous mass of humanity. The criticism is well taken, but let's never forget that numbers are all multiples of one. One hundred is a hundred ones; a thousand, a thousand ones; so it is possible to be honestly concerned about each one of several thousand ones. We need concern for all.

Consider how often numbers of people were referred to in the book of Acts. In 2:41, "three thousand" were saved; in 4:4, "five thousand" believed; the disciples multiplied and a great company of priests found the faith in 6:7; Acts 9:35 states that "all" in Lydda came to Christ; in 11:21 "a great number believed." And in Acts 16:5 the churches "increased in number." The Bible shows that it is good to report numerical success. There is even a book in the Bible called Numbers! I realize that whether numbers are an indication of success or not is relative to the area. Some who are reaching more than others still ought to be doing more because of the greater opportunity they have. The point is that we ought to reach every one we can wherever we are.

This was written anonymously by a Sunday school teacher. Do read it because it illustrates the value of being concerned about a number of individuals.

Shall We Strive for Numbers?

Someone recently said, "I am not interested in numbers. I would rather have a spiritual Sunday school than a big one."

I found myself agreeing and determined to pray and prepare my lesson unusually well for next Sunday. At least my class would be a *spiritual* one. I didn't send the usual little cards as reminders to the class; nor did I visit any prospect; I just let them go, but *I did have my lesson well prepared.* And then came Sunday.

David was absent. Had his dad, so recently saved, taken him fishing again? Were they slipping away from Sunday school and away from God? My heart felt a sharp jab of pain. Jimmie wasn't there. Could he be sick again? What about Charles? Did he ever get those new shoes and was he sitting out on a woodpile feeling "blue" because he didn't make it to Sunday school?

I gave my well-prepared lesson. But those three— what good did it do them?

This week I sent them the prettiest cards I could find. I called them on the phone. I even visited them.

The constant cry in my heart is, "God, don't let them slip away and grow up in sin and careless living. Please, God, bring them back."

Shall we strive for numbers—Yes, O yes! When it is *my* boys, let's have numbers—all eleven of them!

Numbers are only important because they represent individuals who need to be reached for Christ. Surely all of us need to have a greater compassion for more of the lost and unchurched who are so far away from God and will never be brought in unless we go after them. If my house were on fire while I was gone, I would not want my neighbor to be comforted with the fact that he had only gotten one of my children out. That would be good and I would be grateful, but I would want him to rescue all three of my sons and my wife. God is grateful when we win one, but he wants more and more of his created children to become children of redemption. That's the task before us.

However, numbers do become a problem. The problem lies in the fact that often numbers are quoted to give a picture of success when really the success has been far less than reported. Competition often causes a looseness in the accuracy of numbers for statistical boasting, and that is wrong.

It's easy to see how this becomes a subtle substitute, because the numbers give a false sense of achievement, and pride is taken in an inaccurate report—and the lost still remain lost. It's not numbers we're after—it's a number of people. Figures can't get to heaven, only twice-born people. Too often large reported numbers have been substituted for a sincere effort to pay the price of genuine and lasting evangelism. Satan then becomes the victor.

PARACHURCH CLAIMS

Several parachurch organizations have made religious headlines across the country. All Christians should be thankful for the good work they are doing to reach the lost. The church has learned much from these organizations that have greatly benefited ministry. At times, however, exorbitant claims of thousands of conversions come through reports of work on college campuses or in special citywide evangelistic campaigns.

One such well-known group sponsored a city-by-city national campaign "to evangelize America." The organization reported fantastic numbers of conversions, and I hope the figures are totally accurate. Several Christian magazines took a serious look at these claims and found no verification at all, however, for the figures. They found that in many cases "contacts" were reported as salvation experiences.

They obviously are not the same.

One large church of several thousand members got involved in this saturation evangelism campaign. The church had workers involved and gave money to the general budget. One of the members of this good group said that this particular church had "several hundred" accept Christ. The pastor later testified, "If we did, I have yet to see one down the aisle of my church."

Do I believe these people are lying? Not at all. It is, though, a careless handling of the records and the reports in a desire to present a successful campaign. These people are genuinely concerned that all people accept Christ. I believe that. The problem arises when a yes on the telephone is counted when no more contact is made with that person even though further contact was suggested.

Another parachurch group does not conduct these campaigns, but it speaks heavily of discipleship, Scripture memory, and devotional life. Certainly all those things are needed in every Christian's life. Many of these people report how many they have "witnessed to this past week." Once again, however, when pressed about where the converts are, they seem vague in their reply. Yet the very ones who seem so concerned about discipleship don't even lead the ones they have won into the greatest discipling force on earth—the church of Jesus Christ.

Here then lies the problem. The parachurch groups are not equipped to properly evangelize and disciple. They are not even qualified to do the first thing a Christian needs, baptism. That's the job of the church. Yes, I know that others evangelize because the church has failed to do it adequately. I've already said that the church has learned much from these groups. Maybe then this is the function of these groups—to awaken and benefit the church. If this is true, then more of their efforts need to be expanded *through* the church, not just trying to get the church to support their programs.

Too, they must make every effort they can to involve their many converts in the life of the fellowship of God's people, the church. Of course, some of the parachurch people are not active and loyal in a church themselves, so this matter first needs to be resolved before they can genuinely help others.

Christ did not create a group to be known as "Christians Anonymous." He wants every Christian to be a church member. A baptized, faithful, loyal, witnessing, working, tithing church member. "The church," says McGavran, "or rather the Christians, are the very ones who are evangelizing the world. Para-church organizations—like interdenominational missionary societies—rest on the church. The churches support them. The churches pray for them. The churches generate the young people who dedicate their lives to the propagation of the gospel. Back of every successful missionary, there is usually a church in which he grew to Christian manhood or Christian womanhood. The successful missionary, as he goes abroad, begins new churches. The role of the church in the evangelization of the world is very great."[1]

Some of these other groups defend themselves by saying that they are one of the "arms of the church." What good is an extra arm if it slaps the body now and then? Arms are to be a natural part of the body, not casually sewed to the form. It might be better for them to determine to be a part of the heart. That would strengthen the body as a whole.

Spurgeon said it as only he could:

I am weary of this public bragging, this counting of unhatched chickens, this exhibition of doubtful spoils. Lay aside such numberings of the people, such idle pretense of certifying in half a minute that which will need the testing of a lifetime. Hope for the best, but in your highest excitements be reasonable. Inquiry rooms are all very well, but if they lead to idle boastings they will grieve the Holy Spirit, and working abounding evil.[2]

When claims of great numbers of conversions are reported, all Christians should rejoice. But what a tragedy it would be if false claims of success made us relax in our commitment. I thank God for any group or any person who wins others to Christ, but the church has the surest way of making certain the convert is not only won but also discipled into the likeness of our Lord.

ADD-ONS

One pastor said upon his acceptance of a position with a new church, he was excited to hear of their rapidly growing Sunday school. He sat down with the educational director for a long visit about how the Sunday school was reaching so many new people. It really wasn't as exciting as he thought it would be, but it was much more revealing than he had anticipated.

The educational director showed him the basic Sunday school attendance, which was several hundred below the average he had heard about. Then the picture was made clear. Added to the actual attendance were several additional groups. One was an Auditorium Class, which consisted of a hundred (whether counted or not) people who arrived early for the church services. They were not taught or even spoken to for that matter. Another was called the Walking Class. Fifty people were arbitrarily added to the attendance because it was assumed that about fifty people were out walking in the halls who were never really counted in Sunday school. Then there were the two hundred added each week for Bible studies in the home. Of course, no report of attendance was given, and after a close examination, it was discovered that fewer than one hundred had been attending these weekly studies. The most shocking of all to the new pastor was to discover that 10 percent was added to the Sunday school attendance each Sunday "because surely that many were here who were not counted." He soon understood the rapid growth or at least the rapid increase in numbers.

This is an actual case but it is by no means typical. Neither is it unique. There is nothing wrong with having classes at different spots around the church property and counting them, but to add unsubstantiated numbers is not right at all. And surely weekday studies ought not to be included; what is to be reported is the attendance in Bible study for that day.

I do not relate this to squelch creativity in Bible teaching at all. All of us need to think of different approaches to reach people for Christ. A church had one of its adult men's classes in a nearby drugstore that was closed on Sunday. The class was started with just one member and a teacher. That class now has an average attendance of more than forty men.

None of them had been attending Sunday school anywhere. Also, eighteen of that forty were won to Christ and have been baptized by the pastor of the church. These men had prejudices about churches, but they were willing to go to a drugstore, drink free coffee, and have Bible study. Now they are falling in love with church as they better understand it.

A singles group in Dallas, Texas, met for Sunday school once a month at a local motel restaurant. They would eat breakfast and then study the Bible for about forty-five minutes. They reported that literally hundreds were reached for the regular Sunday school by going to the restaurant once a month. It became the net by which many were drawn into the more conventional activities of the church. This is good.

When I became pastor of First Southern Baptist Church of Del City, Oklahoma, there was an X-rated theater about seventy-five yards from our property. Not only was that disturbing, but also the titles on the marquee were too vulgar to mention. You didn't have to go to the movie to have thoughts, just to read the titles on the marquee was sufficient. One day I walked over to the theater and asked the manager if he would mind not putting such titles on that marquee so near our church; He raised up very quickly from cleaning the hot dog machine and said, "Preacher, I don't tell you how to run your church, don't tell me how to run my theater." He was one of those pleasant fellows. I said, "Okay, just thought I would ask."

I discovered that the theater was owned by a large company in our state, and our church arranged to buy the theater. I walked in one day after we had purchased the theater and said to the manager, "Shake hands with your new boss." He said, "Preacher, what are you talking about? Get on back to your church." I told him, "We just bought this theater, and by the way, you're fired." Certainly, we gave him a two-week notice.

After we purchased the theater, we showed C-rated movies—Christ-rated. On Sunday afternoon we would show a free movie and give a Bible lesson to sometimes as many as six hundred young children. Even though we didn't give an invitation, there have been several saved and several parents have been brought to Christ and the church.

There are many creative ways to reach people for the study of the Bible. There is one thing for sure: The best idea has not been thought of yet. There is really no reason to fabricate numbers because if we will work as Christ told us to work, the people will be reached. They are out there, and they are hungry for the gospel.

MINISTERIALLY SPEAKING

We preachers have been accused of speaking "ministerially," which means we exaggerate or stretch the truth, especially when we are reporting church attendance. Most of us would have to admit at least some guilt on this point.

One preacher was asked, "How many do you average in Sunday school?" He replied, "Well, we used to run about seven hundred until some nut counted them." Sometimes, when the actual counting is done, there are not quite as many as we had estimated.

Two pastors were reunited at an annual Southern Baptist Convention, having not seen each other since seminary days. Pretty soon, one asked the other the inevitable question, "What does your church run?"

"Oh, between seven and eight hundred," came the reply.

Astounded at such success, the first pastor inquired, "Well, how many did you have in church last Sunday?"

Sheepishly he replied, "About forty-five."

"Wait—you said you run between seven and eight hundred!"

"Well, forty-five is between seven and eight hundred!" came the reply. It is amazing what we do to impress people.

Most preachers don't do this, but one can make it appear that all preachers are guilty. I overheard a preacher tell a friend that they had more than three hundred one night at a special Bible conference. I was there that particular night, and there were not more than seventy-five present. That's quite a discrepancy.

Let me repeat something I said earlier. Preachers are the finest group of people I know, and the matter of "ministerially speaking" has been made a bigger thing than it is. But what produces the desire to exaggerate? Several things are involved.

One is the desire to do the job God wants us to do, so we report success whether it is always there or not. Preachers want to do God's will. We want to build the church of Jesus Christ. We want to reach people for Bible study.

Another reason is competition. We see someone else doing good, and we want to do good. So, there may be an occasion when we estimate instead of count a particular group. All of us can be cured of this motivation by realizing that bigness is not the only indication of success. Sometimes bigness is not an indication of success at all. Success is being what God wants you to be where you are. Some pastors of small rural churches work as hard as those in the big metropolitan areas where numbers are easier to come by. God knows that these smaller churches away from the population centers need a pastor as much as the city churches do.

Here is the danger in ministerially speaking. It gives a false sense of success. It says that statistics are all-important whether they represent people or not. That could encourage some to find more devious ways to count instead of learning every way possible to reach every person possible. There is no reason to rejoice in a crowd if indeed a crowd is present. Really, the worst thing about it all is that it's not speaking the truth. We preachers need to watch that.

Should we go after numbers then? Certainly, if you're in an area where people are. Go after them. Sometimes the church I pastored was referred to as a "big church." That really wasn't so. There are 500,000 people in our county who do not regularly attend church. For a church to be considered large in the midst of all those unchurched, it should average more than a hundred thousand in attendance. The masses don't come so we can't call ourselves pastors of large churches until we have done a better job of reaching the teeming multitudes who never enter our churches. We really can't accuse anyone of trying to build too big of a church.

Only 8 percent of Americans attend church on a regular basis. Therefore we mustn't fault anyone for being too concerned about reaching a number of people, because no one is even making a dent in the huge sea of lost people all around us. Each of us needs to do more to win every person possible to a saving knowledge of Jesus Christ.

One question has always plagued me: If the people out there are lost, why haven't we reached more of them? Friends, if they are not in our churches, they ought to be. If they are not saved, they ought to be. We must do everything we can do to reach as many people as we can. These are ones for whom Christ died, and they need to be brought to the blessed cross of Calvary. Don't be afraid that you're going to reach too many of them. No one is guilty of that.

Let's quit counting unless there is really something to count. Converting is the issue. Let's get busy about winning millions of precious people to Christ—not to count them but to love them and save them for heaven's sake. Then they will really count—for eternity.

11

JESUS EXCITEMENT WITHOUT CHRISTIAN COMMITMENT

Today we observe a strange phenomenon: Young people are wearing stacked-heeled shoes, tie-dyed shirts, and suede vests. Why is this strange? Because this was the popular look in the seventies. The so-called retro movement reminds me of the excitement around the Jesus movement of that day when multitudes of teenagers were changed from drugs to Jesus.

One could find people wearing Jesus T-shirts, Jesus hats, Jesus hair, and Jesus sandals, as well as an array of crosses, pins, pendants, and emblems. I was very pleased with that movement and regret that more churches didn't do more to conserve the results of the enthusiasm created in those days.

It seems that many young people today are exhibiting a

similar excitement, with the WWJD bracelets and True Love Waits rings.

As is true in any good cause, a movement comprised of outward actions can be imitated by those who have never had the inward experience. The charismatic movement was given impetus through this mistaken external excitement.

This needs to be understood. Jesus said, "Not every one that saith unto me, Lord, Lord, shall enter into the kingdom of heaven; but he that doeth the will of my Father which is in heaven" (Matt. 7:21). There are many today who are saying "Lord, Lord" and "Jesus, Jesus" but are not doing the will of the Father. They generate all kinds of excitement, but there is no apparent commitment. We even hear of so-called revival movements that emphasize such things as being "slain in the Spirit" over the preaching of the Cross!

Let's look at a man in the Bible from whom we can draw our emphasis, and then we'll take a look at the emotionalism that is thrust into today's spotlight. It is possible to have Jesus excitement without Christian commitment. This can become a subtle substitute for real evangelism.

THE MAN WHO WORE THE FIRST JESUS SHIRT

There is a gala party about to begin in a home not too far from Jerusalem on this warm first-century night. As the chariots arrive bringing the invited guests, the dogs can be heard barking in the distance. The sky is beautifully speckled with brilliant stars, and the moon is as large as a golden coin. In back of the home where the party is to be held, meat is cooking over an open fire. The smell, wafted by the wind throughout the neighborhood, intensifies the hunger of all.

Inside the house there is much chatter among the guests as they recount the events of recent days. Suddenly, through the door arrives a man, with his wife by his side, who catches the attention of the other guests. The chatter stops. It picks up again—not about current events, but about the unusual robe the new guest is wearing. "Isn't it beautiful?" "I've never seen one quite like it." "That didn't come from a Jerusalem shop." "It is without seam."

Suddenly someone says, "Where did you get that robe?" The broad-shouldered man turns to the inquirer and says, "This is my Jesus robe. I won it gambling at the base of the cross when we killed that Nazarene sometime ago. You remember." The party continues.

Yes, that's right. The Bible does say that the Roman soldiers gambled for the robe of Jesus. The one that won it surely wore it proudly. He was the first person to ever wear a Jesus shirt, but he was not a follower of Jesus. Let's look more closely at this Roman soldier who wore the first Jesus shirt.

He had the words without the Way. Time and again he must have spoken the name of Jesus. He undoubtedly did at the cross that day as he watched over the crucified there. He said his name every time he explained the presence of such a beautiful robe. No telling how many times he related the story of winning the robe through his unusual skill at dice throwing. Everytime he did, the name of Jesus formed on his lips.

Why, not only did he talk about Jesus but also he used words like the cross, the blood, Calvary, and mentioned sayings such as, "It is finished." He was quite familiar with the

139

words associated with Jesus and his cross. The only problem was, he helped to kill him. He knew the words without the Way. All around us now are those who are just like that. They will use all the right words, but they seem to have lost their way. You can hear them speak, and time and again you will hear not only the name of Jesus but also, "Praise the Lord," "Amen, Brother," "Jesus loves you," "Praise Jesus." The list of such phrases is endless. If said meaningfully and respectfully, there is nothing wrong with those phrases as such.

It is difficult to accept, however, hearing someone say, "Praise the Lord," when a young girl has just agreed to go to bed with him. I once listened to such with a sickened heart as two members of the Children of God cult debated whether they should make love now or later "for Jesus' sake." The giggling, squealing, and embracing mixed with biblical words and phrases made me weep inside. These kids knew the words of Jesus, but they didn't know the way of Jesus. They had taken Jesus and tagged him onto their own ways of filth and immorality, hoping to add credibility to their cheap life style.

It doesn't work. Jesus will not be a part of anybody's program. Jesus is not impressed with our words. He wants our life. He wants us to go his way, not for him to be dragged along behind us as we go our way. Yet there are thousands today who have all the right words but are going the wrong way. They call his name while sipping a cocktail. They call his name while being critical of his church.

Some time ago in California, two young men were killed when the car they were in overturned. The young men were taken to a nearby hospital, but it was too late. A nurse found in the shirt pocket of one of the young men a little familiar verse: "At forty-five miles per hour sing 'Highways Are Happy Ways'; at seventy miles per hour sing 'Nearer My God to Thee'; at eighty-five miles per hour sing 'Lord, I'm Coming Home.'" On investigation it was discovered that the speedometer of the car was locked on ninety-six miles per hour.

The young fellow had the truth over his heart but never into his heart. He knew the words, but he didn't change his ways.

Far too many in our day are using all the right words and doing all the wrong things. Jesus, they need to learn, is not a name to be thrown around; he is life to be caught and a way to be lived. In Salt Lake City, you can see Mormon missionaries wearing WWJD (What Would Jesus Do?) bracelets. The bracelets do not mean there is a changed heart!

A cloak without the Christ is what the Roman soldier had. When the casual observer saw him, they immediately thought of Jesus because he was wearing something that had belonged to Jesus. He was extremely proud of his Jesus shirt, but he didn't know anything about the life of Christ. He had something that belonged to Jesus, but he didn't have Jesus. Wearing a Jesus shirt doesn't make one like Jesus.

What a needy reminder that is. It is all about us. There are those who wear the cloaks of Christ but who have never really met Christ. Jesus taught kindness, love, forgiveness, sharing, thoughtfulness, and benevolence. So many have taken these cloaks to wear for themselves. That within itself is good, but apart from a real experience with Jesus Christ, it is no more than human goodness that leads nowhere. The worst kind of badness is human goodness substituted for the righteousness of Christ. When we stand before God on that day, all of our goodness will be "as filthy rags," but if Christ is in our life it will be his goodness that opens the door of heaven for us.

Many today want to admire the qualities of Jesus but never really sell out to him. Pontius Pilate said he could find no fault in him, but he let the crowd take him and crucify him. He thought he was a good man with good ideas but "away with him," personally. To keep him around may cost too much.

In the South, where I have lived most of my life, it's dangerous not to evaluate your Christianity. Some "come into" the church when they are twelve because it's the thing to do. They are baptized. They join a Baptist church. They like the gospel music, and the pipe organ is wonderful. They have a great admiration for Christ and his church, but for many, Christ is not the Lord and Master of their lives. They love him at a distance. That is, they proudly wear the cloaks of Christ whether he is really their Lord or not because in the Bible Belt it is the thing to do. Many have accepted an atmosphere of Christian culture rather than the lordship of Jesus of Nazareth. They have the trappings of Christianity but not the trust of the Christ himself. They admire Jesus but don't really obey Jesus.

Friend, Christ does not want your admiration; he wants your life. Admiration is not to be a substitute for dedication. Christ does not want to be a thread in the garment of your life; he wants to be the pattern. He doesn't want to be the caboose you hook onto your life; he wants to be the track down which you run.

Written anonymously on the walls of a medieval castle

were these words that all would do well to read:

> You call me Master and Obey me not
> You call me Light and See me not
> You call me Way and Walk me not
> You call me Life and Desire me not
> You call me Wise and Follow me not
> You call me Fair and Love me not
> You call me Rich and Ask me not
> You call me Eternal and Seek me not
> You call me Gracious and Trust me not
> You call me Just and Fear me not
> If I condemn you, Blame me not.

Those who have the cloak without the Christ are not only among the Jesus people and the people of the Bible Belt, but they also are found wherever people try to take what belongs to Jesus without taking Jesus. It's good to have those motions that belong to Jesus, but it's better to have the life that belongs to him. That comes from the experience of being born spiritually when you ask him to enter your life and take complete control.

The crowd without the commitment was another characteristic of the man who wore the first Jesus shirt. This Roman soldier was surrounded by people, as you can imagine, especially after he had the robe of the most celebrated executed criminal in his career. He was well known and wherever he went I imagine people would ask him to share a word or two about Jesus. "Tell us about that time you gambled at the foot of the cross and won that robe," they would insist. Over and over again he told his Jesus story to whomever would listen. Crowds would gather to hear him and see his seamless robe. His Jesus shirt afforded him more friends than he had ever known before the Crucifixion.

Across our land young teenagers and others are parading their Jesus shirts. Some say, "You have a life to live. Jesus has a lot to give." Others say, "No Jesus, no peace. Know Jesus, know peace." Still others say, "I'm high on Jesus." And on cars across America, you see the Christian ichthus symbol of the fish.

Thousands of young people will gather for a concert. Hundreds will meet at a Bible conference. They will hold their hands in the air, close their eyes in rapturous ecstasy, and sing songs of Jesus. They have identified with a cause and a crowd. For this any believer should be thankful. Christian worship needs more enthusiasm with simple faith in Jesus Christ and warm love for one another. I repeat that all of us have learned much good from enthusiasts for the name of Jesus.

In the midst of all this, however, I wonder where the life-long commitment is. How many of them will be appointed missionaries for foreign service? How many of them will become lifetime members of our churches and serve in places of leadership? How many of them will become Christian doctors, lawyers, politicians, businesspeople to significantly influence our world for Christ? How many of them will serve as leaders or helpers in our hospitals, children's homes, homes for unwed mothers, or mission centers?

Maybe the answer to each question is thousands! I hope so, but I don't think so because of the apparent lack of appreciation for the institutional church. The institutional church has its problems, but the greatest hope for our world is still the church of Jesus alive and vibrant in this sick day. It will not become that by excitement alone, it will have to come through solid, unflinching commitment to the purpose of Christ. It's possible to be a part of a crowd and know nothing of commitment. It's possible to wear a Jesus shirt and not have a Jesus heart.

I am thankful for all this enthusiasm, but it must be made lasting by teaching the participants the total claims of Christ upon a life. Sometimes enthusiasm can be a substitute for performance. Being a part of the crowd and part of the committed are not always the same.

A friend of mine returning from Russia told me this true story related to him by some of our Baptist friends in Moscow. A group of Christians were meeting in secret for Bible study in a village near Moscow. Suddenly the door of their meeting room burst open, and there stood two Communist soldiers, their rifles with bayonets pointed at the Christians. One of the soldiers said, "We want to be fair about this, so if you are not really committed to this Jesus stuff and you don't really believe the Bible, we will give you a chance to leave. Now get up and go if that's you."

All but six of the more than twenty left the room in fear for their lives. Then the soldiers went to each of the two doors that entered the room and securely locked them. They listened with their ears pressed against the doors for a moment to make sure the insincere ones had gone. Then they took their rifles and leaned them up against the wall and said, "We're Christians too. We just couldn't take the chance. Let's study God's Word."

Whether in the church or among the hundreds of Jesus people on the streets, there must be found that kind of commitment. It's amazing how a severe test of sincerity can cool the enthusiasm and thin the crowd. I've heard people give devotionals on Sunday morning telling how they would be willing to die for Christ, but they won't be back on Sunday night.

Jesus excitement is good and needed, but Christian commitment is an absolute necessity. Don't substitute cheers for deeds, words for the way, or language for a life. Lasting evangelism is the issue.

CHARISMATICS VOID OF CHARISMA

A few years ago I was flying to West Virginia to speak at a meeting. Frankly, I had been negligent in preparing for the speaking engagement, so I pulled down the tray in front of me, put my Bible on it, and began to read and take notes. A gentleman next to me said, "Excuse me, but are you charismatic?" I thought I would have a little good-natured fun with him and, meaning no harm, I said, "No, I feel fine. How are you?" He said, "No, I mean have you been filled with the Holy Spirit and spoken in tongues?" The discussion continued along those lines all the way to Charleston without either of us changing the mind of the other.

This new kind of thinking that says you must speak in tongues to be filled with the Holy Spirit has made a tremendous impact on modern theological thought. The Bible knows nothing of it. For instance, Paul stated that all the Christians at Corinth (1 Cor. 12:13) had been baptized by the Holy Spirit. He stated seventeen verses later in the same chapter that not all of them spoke in tongues. There is not one verse in all of the Bible that says to be filled with the

Holy Spirit or baptized by the Holy Spirit you have to speak in tongues. Ephesians 5:18, while telling all of us to be filled with the Holy Spirit, fails to mention that speaking in tongues is the way for that to happen.

The purpose of this book is not to give a detailed study of the work of the Holy Spirit. There are dozens of good books on that. My purpose is to show that some emphasize the Holy Spirit in a way that provides just one more substitute to keep Christians from evangelism. This has been one of the more attractive substitutes because one can get into it and seem so spiritual at the same time. In fact, many of the people who seek such things as speaking in tongues are fine, sincere followers of the Lord Jesus.

However, let me make these observations. No place in the Scripture is anyone encouraged to speak in tongues. No place! Not one. It is only mentioned as being in the church at Corinth, and that is the church Paul saw as carnal (1 Cor. 3:1–3). It was considered a troublesome problem in the churches. After Paul wrote the Corinthian letter, he wrote the books of Romans, Galatians, Philippians, Colossians, Philemon, Ephesians, 1 Timothy, 2 Timothy, and Titus without ever referring to tongues. If he had thought the Corinthian experience was good, he certainly would have mentioned it to the others he wrote to after the Corinthian problem.

The word *charismatic* comes from the basic Greek word *charis,* which means "grace." Paul used a plural form of the word in the oft-noted twelfth chapter of 1 Corinthians. *Charismata* referred to the gifts of the Spirit or "grace gifts." These are gifts God sovereignly bestows upon Christians to do the work he has designed for us to do. They are not to call attention to themselves. They are not given because of our goodness. They cannot be earned. I repeat, the charismatic gifts are given to enable Christians to do their work. Dr. W. A. Criswell is correct when he says, "These gifts are God's enablement for his disciples to evangelize the world."[1]

The New Testament was not experience-centered; it was centered in the content of the message of Jesus Christ.

Some time ago a lady told me about attending a "great Holy Ghost" meeting. She was deeply involved in a charismatic group. I said, "Great. What happened?" She said, "Oh, people spoke in tongues. One man had his leg lengthened. Another man had a tooth filled with gold. Also three ladies got the slaying of the Spirit."

"Slaying of the Spirit," I said. "What's that?" She explained, "Well, these ladies came to the pulpit area and the minister hit them lightly with the heel of his hand and they fell down as if they were dead—motionless." She continued, "Now sometimes when they fall their dresses go up over their knees pretty high, but we have a man called Minister of the Blankets who puts blankets over their legs when that happens."

I said to myself, *That's not a great Holy Ghost meeting; that's a circus*. What a disgrace to the precious work of God's Spirit.

I'll tell you what a great Holy Ghost meeting is—it is when a lot of people are saved. The Bible says the Holy Spirit has come to convict of sin, of righteousness, and of judgment (see John 16:7–11). Jesus said that the primary work of the Holy Spirit is getting people to be born again. "No man can come to me, except the Father which hath sent me draw him" (John 6:44).

In John 14, Jesus said something that I could not understand until recently. He said, "Greater works than these shall [ye] do" (v. 12). I just couldn't accept the fact that I could do greater works than Jesus. Then I discovered that John 14 is the chapter in which Jesus told of leaving to us the Holy Spirit. He said that if he stayed we could not receive the Holy Spirit, so he left that all people might have him by the way of his Spirit, and he wouldn't be limited by geographical location by remaining in the flesh. Jesus explained that it is through the power of the Holy Spirit that we can go and share the good news with others.

Now, don't miss this! He then said that better than the blind seeing, Lazarus being raised from the dead, water being turned into wine, or walking on the Sea of Galilee are men and women, boys and girls around the world being saved by the presence and power of the Holy Spirit. Evangelism is better than all the miracles Jesus did—he said so himself. Being a soul-winner is a greater gift than being able to raise the dead.

Isn't it strange that some television preachers can pack giant auditoriums across America through their healing meetings? Crowds gather to see the great things that are happening. Yet the same crowd wouldn't walk across the street to hear a man of God proclaim salvation by grace, resulting in hundreds being saved. It's a pitiful truth that there is a carnal desire for the spectacular. Many of the programs are good and will enrich anyone who watches them. It is certainly to be preferred over what else can be watched on the television screen. It is disturbing, though, how the programming focuses on the mystical, rarely mentioning service or soul-winning. I suppose it's because people's fancies aren't tickled by hearing of a drunkard getting sober and Christ bringing his home back together or a banker on his way to hell giving his life to Jesus or a college student hooked on agnosticism who discovers that Christ is really the Way. A *Star Wars* flavor makes it more appealing.

I watched a Christian television station for more than six hours once, and at no time did anyone mention leading another person to Christ. One man did tell how his spirit left his body and he stood three feet away watching his own body lie on the ground. He said he was in that state for about fifteen minutes, and it was during that time that God spoke a special word to his spirit. I could hardly see any spiritual value in that.

Please understand that I have some dear friends in the charismatic tradition. Many do preach the gospel of Jesus. I have learned some good things from them about praise and joyful worship. My purpose here is not to criticize the charismatic movement any more than I have the hundreds of other things that become substitutes for getting after the souls of people. I'm harder on the Baptist substitutes.

Paul had a good word to say about getting sidetracked even by spiritual things that may lead us away from the Head, Christ Jesus: "Let no man beguile you of your reward in a voluntary humility and worshipping of angels, intruding into those things which he hath not seen, vainly puffed up by his fleshly mind, and not holding the Head" (Col. 2:18–19).

You see, the charismatic movement's excuses, emphasizing phenomenon over the person of Christ, can be used for another subtle substitute for evangelism. Too many people would rather ooh and aah over a supposed miracle than speak a word of love to a lost and needy friend. I certainly believe in miracles both in Bible days and today, and the greatest miracle of all is the miracle of grace as it redeems the lost.

When I went to serve a church in eastern Arkansas, one of the deacons said to me the first week I was there, "Preacher, we hear you like to win folks to Christ. That's fine. We've got a lot of lost people around here, but don't witness to James Smith."

I said, "Why not James Smith?"

"Because," the deacon said, "he hates preachers. One time he hit a preacher square in the face with his fist. Another time he pushed a preacher from his porch so hard the preacher broke his leg."

I said, "You know, I believe you're right; I don't need to visit James Smith."

After about a year the Lord really put it on my heart to visit James Smith. I asked the Lord the second time, and he assured me it was James Smith he had in mind. So I drove my little car to the man's house, got out, walked up the stairs of the porch, and knocked on the door. No one answered. I knocked again and no one came. Finally, I saw that the screen was sticking out a little from the door so I began to hit it so it would bounce back and forth with a loud clatter.

Slowly the door opened and there stood James Smith. He was a truckdriver and had driven all night from El Paso, Texas, and I had just gotten him out of bed. There he stood in an undershirt with hair liberally pouring out over the top. I hate that.

He said, "What do you want?"

I thought I would add a little levity to the situation. I

151

said, "Avon calling." He didn't laugh. I said, "James, I'm the pastor of your wife and daughter, and I've come to tell you how to get saved."

He said, "Come on in."

In less than an hour, James Smith and I were on our knees, our elbows on his couch, and he was giving his heart to Jesus. His wife came in shortly and I said, "Marie, I want you to meet your new husband. James just got saved." Oh, they embraced and wept.

As they were hugging and rejoicing, their little daughter, Frances, came in a side door and put her schoolbooks on the dining room table. She looked over and saw her mother and father crying and embracing. I said, "Frances, your daddy has just been saved." Frances had had polio when she was small, and she wore a metal brace from just above her left knee all the way down under her foot. When she realized what I had said, she hobbled faster than she ever knew she could toward her father, every step making the sound of clanging metal. She reached her little arms up as high as she could to hug her father and said, "Oh Daddy, I've been praying you would get saved. I've been asking Brother Smith to come see you. Oh Daddy, I'm so happy you know Jesus like Mother and me."

The following Sunday James came to our little church and made his decision public. Three other men were also saved that Sunday. What a service we had. What a work of the Holy Spirit.

Friends, that's better than speaking in tongues, having teeth filled with gold, slaying in the Spirit, or legs lengthened. That's a real charismatic service—where God's grace has brought men to the saving knowledge of his Son.

Yes, the new charismatic movement has helped us to get back to emphasizing the Holy Spirit as some have suggested. And, we certainly need to remember that Christianity is an experience to be lived. But remember that the greatest work of the Holy Spirit is convicting the lost of their need of the Savior. Also, remember that any movement that puts the Holy Spirit at its head is in error, for Jesus said that the Holy Spirit is to bear witness not of himself but of the Christ (John 16:13–14).

Man's greatest need is still Jesus. Every Christian's responsibility is to meet that need through daily verbal witnessing. Don't seek an experience to edify self, but seek a soul to glorify God.

12

THE POWER OF
PROPER PRIORITIES

There is only one reason Jesus died, and that's because there is a literal hell. I made that statement in the message I preached in Dallas during the Southern Baptist Convention. A pastor of one of our larger churches came to me and said, "You just changed my life. I'm going back and make the emphasis in our church evangelism so the death of Christ will not be wasted. I've never really thought of that before."

It's true—Jesus only died because there is a hell to escape and a heaven to gain. A church that emphasizes something more than evangelism is frustrating the purpose of the death of Christ. Maybe you object by saying, "Yes, but Christ also fed the hungry, clothed the naked, taught principles of human relationships, and so forth." That's true, friend, but those are all things he did as a living man and teacher. Had God wanted his people to be involved primarily in communicating the principles and ethics of the teachings of Christ, he would have allowed Jesus to teach until he was eighty-five and brought him to heaven on a soft white cloud. The agony of the Cross could have been avoided if God meant for us to emphasize something besides redemption. Christ was the Lamb slain in our stead, and without his death all people would have had to go to hell.

There is no argument at this point. Jesus died to be our substitute on the cross. Had he not done so, we would have had no sin offering and would have had to die in hell ourselves. We could not have been redeemed, bought, and paid for by the life of Christ; it took the death of Calvary. The Calvary part is not just theological verbiage, for Jesus could not have been our Savior just by dying—it had to be a bloody death. "Without shedding of blood is no remission [of sin]" (Heb. 9:22).

If we preach Jesus as example, Buddhism can produce Gautama as their example. If we preach Jesus as teacher, Islam can produce Muhammad who taught truths similar to Jesus'. If we preach patriotism, Shintoism can put us to shame. But there is no one who can be Savior and Redeemer other than he who graced Golgotha's crest.

Too few pulpits today preach this basic truth of the gospel. Preachers have wanted to be known as clever manipulators of homiletical skills or polished orators verbally scanning the contemporary scene. They quote every noted author but quote very little the only One who can permanently bring peace. The great preacher of old finally woke up to this poor stewardship of preaching time and said something I wish every preacher in the world had engraved on his pulpit, "Yesterday I preached my much learning and all the scholars came up and praised me. Today I preached Jesus Christ and him crucified and all the sinners came up and thanked me."

In one of the greatest volumes of sermons ever published, James Stewart says as only he can:

> It must be the most hopeless, sterile, soul-destroying thing imaginable to have only arguments, advice, and moral points of view to offer to the world to help it in its troubles; but to have Christ to offer—a living and accessible and all-sufficient Christ, how different that is, how redemptively effective, how gloriously charged with hope![1]

I heard Billy Graham comment on one of Paul's statements in Romans: "I am not ashamed of the gospel of Christ" (1:16). He said the word *ashamed* meant "embarrassed." "Paul then was saying that he was not embarrassed to preach the simple gospel story," Billy Graham pointed out. He wanted to inspire more than impress.

Read these words of Dr. Stewart:

> Gospel, as everyone knows, means tidings, news, good news. Not views, mark you, but news. The substitution of views for news is one of the most damaging and deadening things that can happen to religion. Sometimes the church itself has become infected by this error, and has been so preoccupied with man's views of God that there has been little time or energy left for heralding God's news to man. What is the news?
>
> "There is only one piece of news I know," said a good

woman to Tennyson, when the poet on a journey had arrived at her house and inquired if anything of note were happening. "There is only one piece of news I know: Christ died for all men." "Well," said Tennyson, "that is old news, and good news, and new news." Is that not your own feeling every time you open your New Testament? Like the great runner Pheidippides, bringing to Athens the news of the victory of Marathon. Those men and women of Jesus were carrying a message from the battle fought out to finish at Calvary; and wherever they passed, through city street or highland glen, one cry they had to all they met, "Tidings, good tidings! The greatest of all good tidings—God and sinners reconciled!" And hearts by the thousands hearing it, were thrilled. It was glorious news, the like of which they had never listened to before.[2]

Too many preachers are not content to preach that. They are not messengers of God's eternal truth but spokesmen for philosophical speculations and worldviews. No wonder half-empty churches with even emptier people are dying. No wonder church members remain lost, never having a genuine experience of salvation. They have lost the power that comes from proper priorities.

Charles McKay said it well,

Pulpits need to be filled with men who have a passion for souls. Moses, who was willing to be blotted out of God's book for the salvation of his people, had it. Jeremiah, who wished that his head were waters and his eyes a fountain of tears if by weeping he could save an apostate people, had passion for souls. Paul, who was willing to be accursed from Christ if at such cost his kinsmen according to the flesh could be saved, had it.[3]

Then he added, "When New Testament churches preach and teach the simple Gospel of Christ, fervently, constantly, and believingly, it is still the power of God unto salvation to everyone that believeth. Stay on the main line and great numbers will turn to the Lord."[4]

That's what this chapter is about. Instead of pointing out another substitute, I want to emphasize the proper place of evangelism in the total ministry of the church. When evangelism becomes priority, there is power from above.

WHAT REAL EVANGELISM IS

Evangelism is at the heart of all we do. It must be. Jesus said himself, "Joy shall be in heaven over one sinner that repenteth, more than over ninety and nine just persons, which need no repentance" (Luke 15:7). Evangelism makes heaven happy because it is the only hope—absolutely the only hope for sinful people.

A. C. Archibald gets at this truth by saying, "The fundamental problem of man's life lies after all, not in mere intellectual and social maladjustments, but in his violated and shattered relation with God. To get a man back into right relations with His maker involves a passionate and earnest evangelism."[5]

This is why Paul was willing to be stoned at Lystra. This is why Stephen was willing to be martyred. This is why John the Baptist would not compromise his message even though it meant losing his head. People can be changed by the power of Jesus Christ now and receive eternal life. It not only gets them out of hell but it also gets the hell out of them. This is the basic motivating power of the gospel.

Here is the modern mistake. When the weak preacher meets resistance, he dilutes his message. He launches out on some nebulous, intellectual nothing to please the itching ears of his listeners. Paul kept preaching the truth and faced the rocks, but in doing so, he saw people changed by the gospel. Today instead, the gospel is being changed by the world, and a human-edited gospel is worthless to meet the deepest needs of the heart. "Times have changed," someone said. True, but times are not our God. Jesus is Lord, and he is "the same yesterday, and today, and for ever" (Heb. 13:8). We all must see that the gospel didn't fit in the day of Jesus either. If we became like our world, we would have nothing to offer the world. You can't lift people up if you're on the same level as they are. We must stay to the truth; hell is hot, heaven is sweet, judgment is certain, and salvation is only in Christ Jesus. Only then can we lead the world from darkness to light, death to life, and from despair to joy. That's the real thing of evangelism.

In Matthew 7, Jesus said some very remarkable things. In verses 13 and 14 he said, "Enter ye in at the strait gate: for wide is the gate, and broad is the way, that leadeth to destruction, and many there be which go in thereat: Because strait is the gate, and narrow is the way, which leadeth unto life, and few there be that find it." In these verses Jesus said two profound things. Not everyone is going to heaven; more will go to hell than to heaven. Now remember that these are not the words of a weird-haired itinerant preacher ranting under his portable tent. These are the words of Jesus of Nazareth. More people will be lost than saved.

Jesus knew that apart from him there was no hope for mankind. He knew that even though he had the answer most people would not receive it. He believed so strongly in the awfulness of hell for those who reject him, he said it would be better for a man to cut off all his limbs and pluck out his eyes and live life like that than to die and go to hell.

You see, it's the teachings of Jesus and his death that should motivate all of us to be soul-winners. Jesus is not the best way to get to heaven; he's the Only Way. Every church then should not only be an evangelistic church, but it should also be training every willing member to be a personal evangelist. Beecher, who was pastor of Park Street Church in Boston, used to say, "I preach on Sunday, but I have 450 members who take my message on Monday and preach it wherever they go." We must all be about the real thing of evangelism—winning every lost person to a saving knowledge of Jesus Christ. Many will be saved if they are told. People are not more difficult to reach today than they were fifty years ago, but too often Christians are lazier than they were fifty years ago.

Evangelism is what's real about the church. Let's get rid of the ecclesiastical trappings and sanctuary synthetics and discover afresh the power of the priority of what's really real—evangelism.

A PERSON-POWERED MINISTRY

So often I will sit down with my staff and say, "All right, let's do a little people talk." They know that I want them to name individuals or individual families who are apart from Christ that they are concerned about. We will spend an hour or so talking about these people and what it might take to reach them for Jesus. Then we close our meeting with a season of prayer for these people. It is so gratifying to see the particular people we've mentioned walk the aisle of our church and begin growing in Christian discipleship. Let me share with you some of the ways we get to know these people and their needs.

One of the unique ministries of my former church at Del City, Oklahoma, was what we called the Springlake service. Springlake is a local amusement park, and each year after our Vacation Bible School, our church went to the park. We arranged with the park officials for a special rate that day. The last few days before we went there, we handed out to the boys and girls hundreds and hundreds of discount coupons.

People arrived at the park from early morning to late afternoon. They rode the rides, fellowshipped with one another, and drank sodas in the popular shady spots. They brought picnic baskets. Around 6:00 P.M. we gathered under the pavilion and ate together. At 8:00 P.M. we all gathered in the park's amphitheater for an evangelistic service. Our music director, Aubie McSwain, had special groups blasting as loud as possible about fifteen minutes before to draw people's attention. So, not only did our members show up but people also came from the midway to hear the music and see what was going on. Hundreds of people gathered for the service.

I would then preach a twenty-minute message on how to accept Christ. Every year people were saved. One of the genuine aspects of the night was that we gave out the Vacation

Bible School certificates. These boys and girls brought their parents—many of whom were lost.

Let me share just one specific illustration. One year a little girl who visited our Vacation Bible School and accepted Christ brought her mother to the Springlake service, and she accepted Christ there. I baptized both the mother and the daughter, and we all began to pray for the father who was not at all interested. I went to see him at their beautiful home. The reception was cordial, but cool. A new member who made a decision at Starlite went over to see Joe and after two hours led him to Christ. I soon baptized Joe, who is the manager of one of the largest department stores in the most modern shopping mall in our state. He has not missed a service since his conversion, and he is bearing a positive witness for Christ. When he made his decision, I firmly shook his hand and said, "Brother, I am really happy for you." He said, "Preacher, I'm glad you are, but I'm the one that's really happy." He still is.

Let me share another way people-centered evangelism is happening. At Southeastern Baptist Theological Seminary in Wake Forest, students in evangelism classes are involved in servanthood evangelism. What that means is they get together in groups and go into the community showing the love of Christ and sharing the love of Christ.

For example, a group regularly pumps gas at a local gas station for free. When asked why they do that, they reply, "We are showing the love of Jesus in a practical way." Then, they witness. Several have been won to Christ.

Others offer free car washes. People are amazed to receive a free car wash! Once a Hindu man came to Christ through this approach. The first time Dr. Alvin Reid, of the Bailey Smith Chair of Evangelism who introduced this to the seminary, went with students into a Laundromat with quarters to pay for the patrons' laundry, two adults were saved! Students go door-to-door to witness, but as they go, they carry light bulbs to give as gifts. Dozens of other examples could be given, but you get the idea.

I'm merely saying get people centered and watch God bring a new power to your ministry. Be creative. Use your imagination. Think beyond traditional approaches and watch God bless you with a great evangelistic future.

David Brainerd, the self-denying compassionate missionary to the American Indians, said, "I cared not where or how I lived or what hardships I went through so that I could but gain souls for Christ. While I was asleep I dreamed of these things, and when I awoke the first thing I thought of was this great work. All of my desire was for the conversion of the heathen and all my hope was in God."

It was love for people that led Christ to Calvary, and it must be our love for him and the ones for whom he died that gets us concerned about those around us. Without question, people by the score will remain lost unless we go with single-mindedness to tell them of Christ.

I recently had one of the biggest thrills of my life. After I preached at a Southern Baptist seminary, a young student came to me and said, "Do you remember me?"

I said, "I don't think so."

He said, "When you were pastor at First Baptist Church of Warren, Arkansas, you came out to visit my mom and dad and led them to Christ. I want to thank you for coming out that night. I'm now studying for the ministry."

I then remembered that this young man's father was a repairman and had worked on various things around the parsonage. I remember saying to myself, *Bailey, you get up and tell people to witness, but this man has been in your home a half dozen times, and you have not even witnessed to him.* So one night I visited his home and was able to lead Havis Smith and his wife to Christ. They were baptized and immediately began to bring their children to our church. Now, their eldest son, Roland, is a successful pastor.

Several years ago I was asked to preach my well-publicized message "Wheat or Tares" at the Sunnylane Baptist Church in Del City, Oklahoma. The Lord blessed that day with many coming to know Christ as their personal Lord and Savior. One of those saved was the youth director, former outstanding quarterback of the National Champion Oklahoma Sooners, J. C. Watts. He later became United States Congressman from Oklahoma.

In the past twelve years through our crusades, I have seen 106 pastors' wives, 93 pastors, 111 staff members, and 88 deacons come to Christ as Savior. The point is you never know who is unsaved. Satan will tell you not to witness to certain people, but do it anyway. The only people who get upset when lost church members get saved are other lost church members.

What if you witness to people and they are already saved? Will they be offended? No Christian is ever offended by an opportunity to affirm his or her salvation.

People are out there who will be saved. They are everywhere and unless we go, many of them will never be saved. And who can tell the generations of saints that will come from just one visit? One person being won to Christ can lead to thousands of other converts and untold numbers of others being called into the gospel ministry.

Evangelism is not just kind deeds or social concern. Christians will do kind deeds and express concern, but they will most of all be about bringing others to Christ. "But remember," says McGavran, "meeting needs, by itself, is not evangelism. Social action must not be substituted for evangelism. Sheep must be found, brought to the fold, and fed."[6]

Let's get up and get with it. Let's knock on doors for the One who is the door to abundant life and everlasting life. No one is going to tell them unless we do.

A REALISTIC VIEW OF THE TASK BEFORE US

Our world is largely lost. It is not begging for the Savior. It is so engrossed in the evils of the hour it doesn't even have enough spiritual perception to see that it's lost. Every day we awaken there is a smaller percentage of Christians than when we retired the night before. What we are doing is not enough. It's inadequate. It's not getting the job done.

Dr. Drummond is exactly right:

> We can no longer conduct business as usual. The business is the same, but conducting it as usual can spell death to congregations, not to say what happens to the multitudes without Christ. It is as simple as that. I know that this issue has been discussed ad nauseam. But the time for discussion is over. Courageous action is now demanded. If we are in any way to meet the demands of this revolutionary age, something of a counter-revolution must take place within the churches.[7]

So, the task before us demands an all-out effort in at least two areas: the reaching of the lost and the motivation of Christians to be consistent soul-winners. Let's look at those in reverse order. The latter will of course aid the former.

The motivation of Christians is the answer but it is not an easy task. It is estimated, for instance, that only five out of one hundred Christians ever win just one person to Christ in a lifetime. What a terrible and heartbreaking tragedy. Where does the problem lie? Apparently in the Christians' relationship to Christ.

Don't just read what Fish and Conant have to say at this point, let it convict you into action.

> If you are a professed follower of Christ and yet are not out in the field laboring to gather the harvest before the storm comes, the words of the late Charles M. Alexander, the great song leader, are for you. "Anybody who is not doing personal work has sin in his life. I don't care who you are—preacher, teacher, mother, father—if you are not reaching definite people to a definite Saviour at a definite time, or trying hard to do so, you have sin in your life." If this is true—and it is, for disobedience to the Great Commission is sin—what a weight of guilt is resting on a multitude of Christians in the church today.[8]

It is sadly true that most Christians never win another soul to Christ. They are apparently not too impressed with the idea that the gospel is good news for surely if they believed that they couldn't keep from telling it. No Christian, irrespective of his or her other gifts, is excused from being a verbal witness for Christ.

This also is the Christian's source of energy to do more. Read these findings of McGavran.

> There are a lot of tired Christians, and it is perfectly true that much of the load of each church is carried by a small number of people. Yet, when you analyze it, you will find that it is not really tiredness but unsuccessfulness that brings fatigue. If members are trying to induce church growth, but are not successful in bringing people into the church, members tend to feel tired and discouraged. If, on the other hand, their efforts lead others to the Lord and new members to the church, the rewards are tremendous, and rather than feeling tired, they feel exuberant.[9]

J. I. Packer surmised, "Every Christian, therefore, has a God-given obligation to make known the Gospel of Christ. And every Christian who declares the Gospel message to any fellow-man does so as Christ's ambassador and representative, according to the terms of his God-given commission."[10]

Let me repeat a truth too often forgotten. Witnessing is every Christian's responsibility. Escape cannot be found in some other achievement in Christian service. Oh, dear Christian, get hot on the trail for the souls of others.

Because of the increasing masses of the lost, we must put forth maximum effort to reach everyone possible. Every twenty-four hours 146,000 people die and most of them are without Christ. The job we have to do is not just with the existing masses who are dying lost; every twenty-four hours 345,000 babies are born. Will we win those? My denomination wins around 400,000 people to Christ a year, which is less than the number of people born January first and second of each year. At this rate it would take the Southern Baptist Convention four thousand years to win the world to Christ providing no more people were born during these four millennia.

With these figures only casually considered, how could anyone say of another, "He's just too evangelistic"? How can anyone be too concerned for souls to be saved? It's impossible! All of us must pray in earnest that God will stir our hearts as never before to reach all of those around us for the Savior. We've got to be about what church is all about.

I heard one time of a young boy who brought home his report card, which showed an F in spelling, an F in arithmetic, an F in history, and an F in English, but an A in citizenship and deportment. As the father was critically scanning the card he looked up at his son and said, "Great, Jimmy, it looks like you're a neat, well-mannered, stupid kid."

Sometimes it's easy to get the idea that churches are making A's in everything that doesn't matter. We have excelled in all that is unimportant, but in the one thing Christ has told us to do—to win, teach, and baptize—we have flunked out.

Years ago in Kentucky a family in a rural valley had the only radio within miles. On that little crystal-set radio they heard that a tornado was spotted, and it was headed in the direction of the valley. The father sent his young son to warn a family by the name of Renfro of the coming storm and to advise them to get in the cellar. The boy ran out the door and just a few yards from his home he noticed a lone bird on a tree over his head. As some boys will do, he picked up a rock and threw it at that bird, but missed it. After a moment or so the bird came back to that same limb. This time the rock was on target and the little bird fell to the ground.

As the boy was holding the slain bird, he heard a terrible roar and noticed the ominous green-black clouds and in their midst, a swirling tornado. Instantaneously it struck the Renfro house and his horrified eyes saw four bodies thrown as straw out into the thick woods.

The little boy threw down the bird and ran to his home. The father had seen the tornado strike the Renfro home and the family destroyed. As the boy approached the front porch of his home, the father grasped him with his strong hands cupped on each of the shoulders of his son. He said, "Merle, you had plenty of time to warn the Renfro family. Why didn't you?"

He said, "Oh, Daddy, as I was going I saw this bird in a tree and I threw this rock at it. I missed it so I threw another one and hit it and I was just holding the little bird when—" The father interrupted and said, "Merle, what's that on your hand?" He said, "Oh, that's the blood of that little bird." The father said, "No son, that's the blood of the Renfro family that you never told."

I wonder if we too often get busy throwing rocks at birds and families go untold. If so, the words of Ezekiel 33:8 ought to be considered: "When I say unto the wicked, O wicked man, thou shalt surely die; if thou dost not speak to warn the wicked from his way, that wicked man shall die in his iniquity; but his blood will I require at thine hand."

McGavran sees the great task before us and says, "We must equip Christians in the United States to spread the faith to millions. It is not sufficient to bring a few people into our church. The task is to win millions who do not now know Christ to earnest, ardent faith in him. Nothing else will roll back the tide of materialistic, superficial, sinful living."[11]

Let's make as our theme song for this crusade for the Master the third stanza of Heber's great hymn "From Greenland's Icy Mountains."

Can we, whose souls are lighted
By wisdom from on high,
Can we to men benighted
The lamp of life deny?
Salvation! O salvation!
The joyful sound proclaim,
Till earth's remotest nation
Has learned Messiah's name.

13

A HEART HOT
FOR SOULS

As a young boy I remember pastors and evangelists talking about "a burden for souls" or "a passion for souls." Oh, how we need to hear those phrases again from men and women who possess what I call a heart hot for souls.

Someone once said to William Booth, founder of the Salvation Army, "I understand your evangelism program is the very best." He responded, "No, it could be better." "What could be better, General Booth?" they insisted. "If," Booth responded, "all of my soldiers could spend just five minutes in hell that would be the best training for soul-winners."

I'm sure that would be the case, but the Father will never let that happen because we would literally go insane by what we would see. Indeed, it would give us a burden, a passion, and a zeal for the souls of the lost. Surely, however, we should receive an adequate burden by believing without question the Bible regarding the reality of a horrific place called hell where the rejectors of Christ stay forever.

I found interesting what Jim Wilson shared while preaching at First Baptist Church of Arnold, Missouri, during one of the Real Evangelism Conferences sponsored by our ministry. He said that after resigning as pastor of the First Baptist Church of Beaumont, Texas, to reenter evangelism he decided to go to Black Mountain, North Carolina, to visit with Billy Graham. Jim could arrange this because his father, T. W. Wilson, has been Billy Graham's personal assistant and close friend from the beginning of his ministry.

There in Billy Graham's home in Montreat, Jim asked him if he had any regrets after such an illustrious and effective ministry as the world's most famous evangelist. Would he do anything different? Billy Graham said, "Jim, two things. I would preach on hell more, and second, I would use the term *soul-winner* instead of *witness*."

That is significant from such a great harvester of souls. I agree with him that the subject of everlasting punishment must be preached more often because from that Christians should cultivate a genuine concern for the unsaved. Also, the term *witness* can often let us off the hook by making us believe we have done enough even though it stops short of winning souls to Christ.

In the closing paragraphs of this book, I want to share with you what many with a heart hot for souls have said regarding their passion. I pray that you will read these words time and time again. I do so, and they often bring me to tears and always fan the flame burning in my heart for souls.

The powerful preacher for souls John Wesley said, "Let us all be of one business. We live only for this, to save our own souls and the souls of those who hear us. Give me one hundred preachers who fear nothing but sin and desire nothing but God, and I care not a straw whether they be clergymen or laymen, such alone will shake the gates of hell and set up the kingdom of heaven on earth."[1]

Brother Walters, president of the British Methodist Conference, noted that one Monday morning he went by the office of Hugh Price Hughes to check on his success in establishing churches for the Wesleyan movement. The man looked as if the weight of the world were on his shoulders—obviously downtrodden. Walters asked him if he was sick. He said, "No. Walters, we have had three Sunday nights at St. James Hill without anyone in the inquiry rooms—no conversions—and I can't stand it. It will break my heart. . . . When God sent me to West London, it was that, whenever I preached, I should win a verdict for Christ."

John Hyde, known mainly as "Praying Hyde" the last several years of his missionary ministry, averaged leading four souls a day to Christ. His daily prayer was, "Father, give me souls or I die!"

And read the words of these two men hot for souls. James Caughey said, "Oh, to burn out for God! All, all for Him! Jesus only! Souls! Souls! Souls! I am determined to be a winner of souls. God help me." John Smith echoed a similar burden when he said, "I am a brokenhearted man; not for myself but on account of others. God has given me such a sight for value of precious souls that I cannot live if souls are not saved. Give me souls or else I die."

George Whitfield, the anointed evangelist and revivalist,

said with his face glowing with tears, "Oh Lord, give me souls or take my soul."

Charles Cowman, founder of OMS International, wrote as his burden for Japan almost overwhelmed him, "By the help of God they shall hear if it costs every drop of my life's blood. Here I am, Lord, send me! Send me!" Others said of him, "The winning of a soul was to him what the winning of a battle is to a soldier; a race is to an athlete. Charles Cowman lived for just one thing—to win souls for Christ. This was his soul passion, and in a very extraordinary manner God set His seal upon it."

John Knox's wife would ask him why he was praying so late into the night and he would say, "How can I sleep when my land is not saved?" And he often prayed, "Lord, give me Scotland or I die!"

The words of Philip Doddridge are indeed inspiring: "I long for the conversion of souls more sensibly than for anything else. Methinks I could not only labor, but die for it."

Bishop Joseph Berry, commenting on the parable in Luke 14 (in which the guests who were invited to supper began to make excuses why they couldn't come and the host commands his servants to go to the streets and invite others), says, "Have you no concern, O happy guests, for the starving ones in the streets? Out, out of the light and warmth! Out into the chilling storm! Out into the dismal streets! Invite them to come. That is not enough. Persuade them to come. That is not enough. Compel them to come! The man who sits down to the banquet and selfishly enjoys its light and warmth, with never a thought of the hungry multitude outside, is a caricature of a Christian. He has caught no true vision of his Lord; nor have the fires of

Christian evangelism been kindled in his heart. He may be a church member, but he is not a Christian. . . . Is anyone a real disciple of Christ who is not swayed by this consuming passion?"

Charles Finney summed up our responsibility when he said, "A Christian is either a soul-winner or a backslider."

These statements of some of God's great men have stirred my heart for years. I have found them in many places, but several were quoted by Dr. Wesley L. Duewel in his classic work, *A Blaze for God*, which I recommend with enthusiasm. I wanted to include these in this volume so they would be available for each of you as you pray for our dear Lord to make you a more consistent soul-winner.

Several times I have been the guest preacher at the great Peoples Church in Toronto, Canada, where my good friend John Hull is pastor. Dr. Hull is keeping the church focused on soul-winning and missions just as the famous founder of the church, Dr. Oswald J. Smith. Read what this dear man said regarding his passion for souls.

> Never will I be satisfied until God works in convicting power and men and women weep their way to the cross. Oh that He would break me down and cause me to weep for the salvation of souls. . . . About two this afternoon I was praying, when suddenly, I stopped and began to praise God. Tears flowed copiously. All I could do was sob out, "They're lost! They're lost! They're lost!" and so I wept and prayed for the people.

My prayer is that Christ will increase my heart cry for souls. To believe the Bible is to believe the destination of those who have never received Christ is horrible and eternal. Even the lost world feels that if we really believed what we say, we would do more about it.

Dr. Duewel illustrated that truth so powerfully in this story:

A notorious British murderer was sentenced to die. On the morning of his execution the prison chaplain walked beside him to the gallows and routinely read some Bible verses. The prisoner was shocked that the chaplain was so perfunctory, unmoved, and uncompassionate in the shadow of the scaffold. He said to the preacher, "Sir, if I believed what you and the church say you believe, even if England was covered in broken glass from coast to coast, from shore to shore, I would walk over it—if need be on my hands and knees—and think it worthwhile, just to save one soul from an eternal hell like that."[2]

A MUST-READ ADDENDUM

On June 4, 1940, with the Germans bombing much of Europe, causing several countries to surrender, Winston Churchill stood before the House of Commons and said that while others may surrender ". . . we shall not flag or fail. We shall go on to the end. . . . We shall fight in the seas and the ocean. . . . We shall fight on the beaches, we shall fight on the landing grounds, we shall fight on the fields and in the streets, we shall fight in the hills; we shall never surrender."

At this time all was set for the battle of Dunkirk. It seemed German ships were everywhere in the English Channel and 350,000 allied troops were poised for war. When Paul Joseph Goebbels heard what Churchill had said, he related it to Hitler and the ruthless dictator ordered the complete withdrawal of German ships. British historians believe that if the battle at Dunkirk had taken place at least 160,000 allied forces would have died.

Preacher, do you get it? One hundred sixty thousand men went home to their families because of what one man said that inspired millions and put fear in the mind and heart of an evil man. PREACHER, SAY SOMETHING. People should leave a church service different than when they walked in—too much of a rarity today in this generation of pulpits filled with clergymen who have ministerial careers instead of gospel messages in their hearts burning to be delivered with power and life-changing conviction.

Preachers have developed the art of almost saying something. The respected Christian writer C. S. Lewis said once he attended a church service where the young, mild-mannered pastor said near the close of his mild-mannered sermon, "The sovereign in Heaven under certain circumstances without your receiving His plan for an alternative may cause you some unpleasant eschatological results." After the service, Lewis said to the pastor, "Were you trying to say that people who reject Jesus will go to Hell?" The pastor replied, "Well, yes." Lewis returned, "Then say so." SAY SO, PREACHER!

If, pastor, you don't have the will or the intention of preaching powerfully, use the vocational evangelist. I heard Dr. Roy Fish say, "Two things which are in a sad state of neglect today are the number of revival meetings held in Southern Baptist churches and the use of vocational evangelists for these meetings. Without a doubt, this is one reason why the number of people baptized in our churches has been declining." Dr. Fish was a long-time professor of evangelism at Southwestern Baptist Seminary in Fort Worth, Texas—the world's largest seminary—and is still preaching in this year of 2012.

Occasionally some pastor will tell me he does not like

"professional evangelists." I say to him, "Do you like professional pastors?" The pastor (and I was one for almost thirty years) needs to know this truth. The word "pastor" is only used one time in the New Testament while the word "evangelist" is used three times: Acts 21:8, Ephesians 4:11, and 2 Timothy 4:5.

To put it in medical terms, the pastor is the general practitioner while the evangelist is the surgeon—the church needs both obstetrics and pediatrics, birth and care.

Dr. Tom Johnston, Ph.D. and professor of evangelism, said it well. He wrote in a work not yet published, *The Work and Worth of the Evangelist*: "So the title 'evangelist' is like a winnowing fork. By its very nature it carries with it a host of presuppositions. God has providentially kept this title very narrowly defined. And for this reason the evangelist suffers the reproach of the Gospel. Those who do not agree with his methodology or his doctrinal position find fault with him. This is certainly why J.M. Carroll said so many years ago when speaking of evangelists, 'Deny not fins to things that must swim against the tide, nor wings that must fly against the wind' (*Baptist Standard*, May 31, 1906). The evangelist is a divine burr under the saddle of the church and culture, keeping both in check." AMEN to that!

ABOUT REVIVAL MEETINGS

In the largest non-Catholic denomination in the world this finding was very revealing. Churches that held revivals had a 24:1 ratio of baptisms to resident memberships. Churches not conducting revivals had a 43:1 ratio. Need I say more?

One of my dearest friends, Harold Mathena, eminently

successful in business as well as in the ministry, said to someone something every reader must remember. Said this man to Harold Mathena, "Revivals don't work anymore." I love what Mr. Mathena said back, "Well they did until we quit doing them."

The truth is that pastors have quit working in this area. If we could get our pastors revived, revivals in the church would happen again with hell-shaking, heaven-rejoicing results. In my ministry now I see more conversions in four days than the church I am in has in a year. ~REVIVAL~

REMEMBER THE WORDS: ALTAR CALL, MOURNERS BENCH, INVITATION

Those were the days. Churches once had trained a godly group of counselors called altar workers. They knew how to deal with a person who had walked the aisle to either be born again or to make a decision for a deeper walk with Christ. Sadly today so much preaching is apologetic and antiseptic no one sees the need to deal with any issues in their lives. The altar worker is as outdated as a kerosene lamp. So I hear on a regular basis, "You know that church doesn't even give an invitation." I think to myself, *You can't have a dessert unless you've had a meal.* Oh dear God, give us once again the kind of preaching that convinces the unbeliever to receive the salvation by grace and troubles the heart of the backslider that he cannot find rest until he repents and begins once again to walk holy before Christ.

I've preached many times in prisons from Florida to Alaska. My attention was brought to highest alert when I read this. A preacher went a day early to a prison where he was to preach to familiarize himself with the facilities. The warden showed him the building where the inmates would gather to hear him preach the next day. He noticed as they walked inside two chairs draped in black to the right of the podium a distance from where every other person would be gathered. He asked the warden about the chairs draped in black and he was informed the two men who would sit in those chairs would be put to death in the electric chair at 6:30 a.m. the day after he preached. The preacher asked, "My sermon will be the last sermon those men will ever hear?" The warden replied, "Yes, it will be their last. They will be dead less than ten hours after your sermon!"

The preacher went home and got alone with God. In tears he prayed, "Dear Father, what I had planned is so anemic and stale. Father, please forgive me for taking my assignment so lightly. These two men deserve more than entertaining remarks. Dear God, please help me preach the Gospel with the promise of everlasting life and your forgiveness through a bloody cross." And his prayer was answered.

One night after I had preached in a football stadium to several thousand, one man who had accepted Christ that evening sought me out to tell me this: "Pastor Smith, our church does not give an invitation and I believe had you not given one tonight I would have never been saved." The next night he walked into a theater to see a live performance of a Shakespeare play, when his estranged wife, who was hidden behind a pillar in the foyer, stepped in front of him and shot him dead.

"Preacher, had you not given an invitation I would have never been saved." That sentence today still makes me wish I could speak to every preacher at one time and say,

"PREACH WITH URGENCY AS IF YOUR HEARERS WILL NEVER HAVE ANOTHER TIME TO TRUST CHRIST."

Dr. W.A. Criswell, by far my all-time favorite preacher, said in the introduction of R. Alan Streett's book: "The preacher is the man of God pointing the way to heaven. As such, the proclaimer of the Gospel ought to preach for a verdict. Moses did. Isaiah did. Jesus did. Paul did. Peter did. For a man to preach for the sake of preaching is a travesty on the truth of God. We ought to preach with a purpose and plead for a response" (*The Effective Invitation*, Fleming H. Revell, 1984).

As I close this volume, I am saddened by the condition of many of our churches to which I am no stranger. We have sanitized our music, neutralized our preaching, compromised our beliefs, fossilized our congregations, minimized our services, and maximized our indifference.

In my denomination in 1950 with 27,788 churches, we baptized 376,085 people. In 2011 with 45,764 churches, we baptized 333,341. Think about it. Almost double the number of churches with fewer conversions.

Do we need more churches? It does not matter how many blades you put on a razor if they are all dull!

Do I believe all of the above to be true because of my age? Yes, I am old enough to remember when we did it right. With God's help, let's do it right again.

NOTES

CHAPTER 1

1. G. Campbell Morgan, *Evangelism* (Grand Rapids: Baker Book House, 1976), 31–32.
2. Ibid., 7.
3. John F. Havlik, *The Evangelistic Church* (Nashville: Convention Press, 1976), 89.
4. Charles L. McKay, *The Call of the Harvest* (Nashville: Convention Press, 1956), 17.
5. Havlik, *The Evangelistic Church*, 67.
6. Win Arn and Donald A. McGavran, *How to Grow a Church* (Glendale, Calif.: Regal, Div. G/L Publications, 1974), 103.
7. Havlik, *The Evangelistic Church*, 18.
8. Ibid., 22.
9. A. C. Archibald, *New Testament Evangelism* (Chicago: Judson, 1946), 42.
10. Arn and McGavran, *How to Grow a Church*, 103.
11. Archibald, *New Testament Evangelism*, 42.
12. Arn and McGavran, *How to Grow a Church*, 80.
13. Havlik, *The Evangelistic Church*.
14. C. E. Autrey, *Basic Evangelism* (Grand Rapids: Zondervan, 1959), 50.

CHAPTER 2

1. F. E. Marsh, *Emblems of the Holy Spirit* (Grand Rapids: Kregel Publications, 1957), 56.
2. H. H. Hobbs, *New Testament Evangelism* (Nashville: Convention Press, 1960), 44.
3. Jessie Penn-Lewis, *War on the Saints* (The Overcomer Literature Trust, England, 1956), 51.
4. Charles H. Spurgeon, *The Soul Winner* (Grand Rapids: Zondervan, 1948), 140.
5. Lewis Drummond, *Leading Your Church in Evangelism* (Nashville: Broadman, 1975), 156.
6. Spurgeon, *The Soul Winner,* 75.
7. Ibid., 75–76.
8. Penn-Lewis, *War on the Saints,* 61.
9. Arn and McGavran, *How to Grow a Church,* 81.
10. Autrey, *Basic Evangelism,* 50.

CHAPTER 3

1. Arn and McGavran, *How to Grow a Church,* 166.

CHAPTER 4

1. Roy J. Fish and J. E. Conant, *Every Member Evangelism for Today* (New York: Harper & Row, 1922), 54.
2. Ibid., 53–54.
3. Ibid., 53.
4. Arn and McGavran, *How to Grow a Church,* 81.
5. McKay, *The Call of the Harvest,* 22.

CHAPTER 5

1. Autrey, *Basic Evangelism,* 91.

CHAPTER 6

1. Arn and McGavran, *How to Grow a Church,* 42.
2. Harold Lindsell, *Evangelism Now* (Minneapolis, Minn.: World Wide Publications, 1969), 34.
3. Robert Coleman, *The Master Plan of Evangelism* (Old Tappan, N.J.: Fleming H. Revell Co., 1963), 109.
4. Fish and Conant, *Every Member Evangelism,* 62.
5. Spurgeon, *The Soul Winner,* 75.

CHAPTER 7

1. Arn and McGavran, *How to Grow a Church,* 103.

Notes

2. Quoted in R. G. Lee, *Bread from Bellevue Oven* (Wheaton, Ill.: Sword of the Lord, 1947), 134.
3. Ibid., 137.

CHAPTER 9

1. McKay, *The Call of the Harvest*, 88.
2. Ibid., 88.
3. Charles Taylor, *Wake Forest Student, March 1916* (Wake Forest, N.C.: Wake Forest College).
4. Arn and McGavran, *How to Grow a Church*, 86.
5. Andrew Murray, *A Minister's Obstacles* (Westwood, N.J.: Fleming H. Revell Co., 1959), 15.

CHAPTER 10

1. Arn and McGavran, *How to Grow a Church*, 38.
2. Spurgeon, *The Soul Winner*, 16.

CHAPTER 11

1. W. A. Criswell, *The Baptism, Filling, and Gifts of the Holy Spirit* (Grand Rapids: Zondervan, 1973), 48.

CHAPTER 12

1. James Stewart, *The Strong Name* (New York: Charles Scribner's Sons, 1941), 95.
2. Ibid., 94.
3. McKay, *The Call of the Harvest*, 24.
4. Ibid., 24.
5. Archibald, *New Testament Evangelism*, 56.
6. Arn and McGavran, *How to Grow a Church*, 107.
7. Drummond, *Leading Your Church in Evangelism*, 19.
8. Fish and Conant, *Every Member Evangelism*, 70.
9. Arn and McGavran, *How to Grow a Church*, 88.
10. J. I. Packer, *Evangelism and the Sovereignty of God* (Downers Grove, Ill.: InterVarsity Press, 1961), 46.
11. Arn and McGavran, *How to Grow a Church*, 86.

CHAPTER 13

1. Oswald J. Smith, *The Passion for Souls* (Marshall, Morgan & Scott, 1965), 167ff.
2. Wesley L. Duewel, *A Blaze for God* (Grand Rapids: Zondervan, 1989), 121.